Market Technique

NUMBER TWO

by

RICHARD D. WYCKOFF

Containing the principal articles, editorials, and correspondence originally published in the magazine Stock Market Technique from August 1933 to July 1934, inclusive

Originally published in 1934
by Richard D. Wyckoff

Copyright © 1989 by Fraser Publishing Company

Second printing, 2003

Library of Congress Catalog Card Number: 84-80545
ISBN: 0-87034-093-X

Cover design by Sherry White

TABLE OF CONTENTS

iv

Flashes

THERE is no sweeter business than trading in stocks when you know how.

I do not deny that the untrained trader may make money. He will at times, but in most cases he will fail to keep it.

What is the best time to buy or sell? At the zoological moment, as they say among the bulls and bears.

Never make a speculative transaction unless the prospective profit is several times the amount of your risk. And limit the risk.

Only those who fail to realize the risk will venture their resources in stock speculation without first learning how.

To treat the stock market as one does betting on the races is to overlook one of the greatest opportunities for legitimate money-making.

Stock speculation conducted under scientific procedure is a reputable and meritorious avocation. It is not gambling; it is using intelligent foresight.

The President of the New York Stock Exchange says this country needs speculators; their stock market operations benefit the community; they aid in creating a broad market.

In attempting to extract profits from the stock market, are you employing sugar-tongs or steam dredges? Are you nibbling a little here and there, or are you scooping out profits in bunches?

The man who *thinks* he knows the stock market is usually his own worst enemy, because in the majority of cases he merely has a large furry ear open for tips. When one of these happens to go right, he flaunts himself on his astuteness.

Trading in Stocks as a Profession

TO MOST of the twenty million people who are in the stock market or holding stocks, trading or investing is an avocation; that is, a casual or transient occupation — a diversion. Many make occasional jabs at the market and look upon these much as they do their race track ventures. Few regard the stock market as an arena where they can, if they will, work out careers for themselves by becoming successful, scientific traders in stocks so that they can abandon all other businesses and professions and devote themselves exclusively to the tape.

The stock market affords the greatest possibilities of almost any field you can name, based on profits that can be realized from the fluctuations. Not only that: The business of trading in stocks can be learned in spare time and started on a trifling amount of money. Most of the big traders we read about began in a very limited way. A student is making progress even while trading on paper, when these hypothetical transactions have been, in the net, successful: when a long series of such trades show more profits than losses. And until he can reach that point he is not justified in venturing real money.

Let us suppose that he has now graduated from the theoretical, imaginary or paper trading to the point where he is ready to make a genuine start. It should be done in a small way. A ten-share lot is ample. A hundred or two hundred dollars is plenty of capital, for the loss of this indicates that he has begun before he is qualified and he should, later, begin again. His progress may be marked by other setbacks — just as in any other business or profession.

When a man tells me he is going to take $10,000, $50,000 or $100,000 and do some trading in the stock market I know what the result will be in the majority of cases. He is like a battleship that sails up to the enemy's forts and turns its broadside. Large capital is a great handicap to anyone undertaking to become a professional trader in stocks. The vast fortunes that melted away from 1929 to 1932 are proof that no amount of money fortifies one against the loss of that amount and more. You can confirm this by inquiring into the records of many leading financiers, or their estates, if they passed out from 1929 to 1932, and the record of lost millions by the so-called "Big Ten" who were the most prominent operators in the '29 boom.

It is pertinent to ask why great accumulations of money, once headed toward the billion dollar mark, so largely disappeared. Bankers, railroad magnates, captains of industry, partners in banking houses, large stock operators, were supposed to know the game. They were more or less on the inside. Why didn't they know enough to sell out in the boom? Why did they buy more too soon — before the depression had run its course? Why were many of them in hock before the market reached the low? I'll say they didn't play the game according to scientific rules. Fortunes in securities locked up in their boxes and to a degree "put away and forgotten" were not protected against shrinkage in market prices. A man's judgment, not his steel vault, must accomplish this for him.

Jay Gould had the right idea: "If the story of the men that Wall Street made rich were written, it would fill several books. If the story of the men that Wall Street made rich *and then broke* were written, it would fill a library. These men who became rich were in almost every case men of ability, good traders, and keen business men, but they overplayed their hands. They knew when to come in, but they didn't know when to get out. The perfect speculator, the perfect gambler, if you will, must know when to come in; more important, he must know when to stay out; and, most important, he must know when to get out once he is in." *

It has been proven that those who should have known most about the stock market and investments failed in the

* Jay Gould-Greenberg, Pub. N. Y.

final test. They did not see this thing coming; they carried all or most of their loads down to the point where they were practically forced to strip themselves of possessions.

A banker of international reputation, who all his life had been piling up millions, went abroad in the summer of 1929. When he had the ocean between him and the Stock Exchange he decided the U. S. was stock crazy. He cabled to his partners to sell everything he had. They replied: "No, don't do that; you're crazy; this thing has just begun." So he sold only a fraction of his holdings. He told some friends how little he had left early in 1933.

A lawyer, with the highest type of banking connections in New York, found at the top of the boom that he had paper profits of a million dollars, mostly made in bank stocks. Seeing the handwriting on the wall he went to his banker-guide to confirm his own decision that it was time to get out. The banker, one of America's leading lights, said: "Don't think of it! There's another fifty percent on your money ahead!" Many other similar experiences are well known, and enough has transpired to prove that it is not the possession of capital but the acquisition of knowledge of the stock market that is the vital point in attempting a Wall Street career.

A great deal depends on the attitude one takes toward the market in the beginning. One man may be content with an occasional flyer, in which he hopes to get away with a profit. Another may try to run a little money into a big stake, like the fellows who play combinations on the races. Others may try to make "a clean-up" and have the supreme satisfaction of one big event in their lives. If a man is looking (as most men are) for income and profit from his so-called investments, that is still another objective.

There is the plunger type of operator who at times stakes all his resources on a single play; who is so cocksure he is right that nothing can induce him to take precautions. He becomes mentally intrenched in a certain position, and burns all his bridges behind him. These plungers go broke frequently. In one month they may have several million dollars and the next month be in debt to their brokers.

Then there is the long pull investor, as he calls himself, who very often knows how to buy right but is not a good seller. Usually his avarice increases with the expansion of his fortune. There is an old chap of this type who makes the Cotton Exchange his headquarters. Among other things he had some 50,000 shares of Southern Railway common for which he was offered a handsome price when the market was high; but he wanted more for these and other holdings. Now he will tell you sadly, "I had eighteen millions but I wanted twenty-five; now I've got only two." In one sense it didn't make any real difference to him whether he had $18,000,000 or $25,000,000, but having set the higher objective for himself, when he lost sixteen out of eighteen he felt that he was comparatively ruined.

In describing these types I merely wish to distinguish them from the trader who considers seriously the possibility of making a profession of trading in stocks, and who hopes to make it pay him so well that he needs no other vocation.

Some of the advantages of trading in stocks as a profession are these: After you have made progress and are developing at least a trace of good judgment, you do not have to depend on anyone else. Even as a small trader you can be as much a lone wolf as a large operator. You need no office, no equipment, no employees, no clients. You have no office hours. You do not have to trade every day or every week or month. You can plan your own time, trading seldom or often. You can take a position in stocks and go away from the ticker; there are certain ways in which the movement of prices may be judged without watching the translux, although there is much to be gained from studying the market constantly — just as a surgeon becomes more proficient by performing many operations.

[*To be continued*]

Who Is an Expert?

IN THE *New York Times* of May 21, 1933, we read the following heading: TIME NOW TO INVEST IS VIEW OF EXPERTS.

The article states that this is "owing to the improvement in business. The experts whose opinions were sought administer funds totalling several hundred millions of dollars. . . . The dominant factor stressed now by the experts is rising activity in trade."

This attitude of the "experts" was published ten months after most securities registered their lows. Last July (1932) the *Times* average of 50 stocks recorded 34. On May 20, this year, they were 74. The Dow Jones Industrials, then 41, had risen to 81. At these bottom prices we do not recall a peep from a single expert. They did not advise the purchase of Telephone at 70, now 112; or Atchison at 18, now 63; or Can at 30, now 85; or General Motors at 8, now 24; or U. S. Steel at 21, now 50. (By "now" we mean May 20th closing prices — the day before the article appeared.) Evidently these "experts" thought it safer (for them) to wait until leading stocks had doubled or trebled in market value before they came out of their cyclone cellars and advised bravely: *Now you can buy them.*

We always regarded an expert as one who knew how to buy at or near the low point of the market. Anyone can see that we were mistaken. Let us, therefore, revise this definition to something like the following: An "expert" is one who waits nearly a year after the low point, when the real bargains were obtainable; who ignores several opportunities to buy on weak spots during the year. An "expert," 1933 model, waits until his newspapers report the steel companies operating at 40% of capacity; until wheat, cotton and all the other commodities are way up from their lows; until recovery is well under way.

An "expert" considers Union Pacific a rank speculation at 27⅝, but a sound investment at par.

By the time the confidence of the "experts" is restored, shrewd buyers may realize from 20 to 70 points profit; but not till then is it safe for "experts" to advise their clients to buy.

Lost profits already amount to hundreds of millions. The blind leading the blind. How do they get away with it?

Technical Position of Woolworth

A BLOCK of 250,000 shares of Woolworth was liquidated as rapidly as the market would take it up to about the middle of May. It is said this stock came mostly from Germany. During this time the stock fluctuated between 35 and 38, which was a remarkable indication of the market's power of absorption. No manipulation was necessary. As demand for substantial lots appeared these were supplied, but the stock held firmly within that narrow range.

Almost anyone knowing in advance that this block of stock was to be sold, might have expected the price to break. Had the liquidation come along a few months earlier, that doubtless would have been the case, because the buying power then was small in comparison with the amount for sale. But as the stock did not break, a strong technical position was indicated. This was confirmed when the selling was completed. Soon after, the price reached 40. Demand was greater than the heavy supply.

Inside information would have said "sell it short" when the selling began. This incident seems to indicate that it matters not whose stock or how many shares are being sold: if buyers outnumber sellers the price of the stock will rise. The law of supply and demand always governs.

Why Ask Advice?

WHY DO you come to me for tips?

Are you always going to stake your money on what someone says is "A good buy?"

And why do you hire people by the month or year to dope out the market for you? Are you never going to develop a judgment of your own?

You don't think you can. Why not? All these people who try to sell or give you advice, at one time knew nothing about the market; now you are patronizing them. An old adage of the Street says· The public will lean on anyone whom they think knows ten percent more about the market.

Even if I were to advise you, I would not really be helping you: I would only be making you more dependent. By refusing to give you tips, I put you on your own resources. Of course I expect if you can't get me to tip you off you'll probably ask someone else for advice; but if you continue to pursue this practice, your stock market career will consist of a series of bets on what someone else told you — a lot of ventures on other people's opinions. Can you really afford to risk your money that way?

Dear Advisory Service: You may be right now, but I followed your advice for three years and all I have left is a seat on the curb.

Should you accept my present opinion, how do you know I may not reverse my attitude within the hour? In that case, am I expected to hunt you up and tell you so? And if I do not, and my revised judgment proves correct, you will then suffer a loss, through no fault of mine, for I did not agree to inform you every time I had a new view of the market.

When you asked me, perhaps I *was* bullish, but now I have reason to be a bear. That is my privilege. Either one position or the other will prove to be the correct one, but whether I am right or wrong in this instance proves nothing. I have been wrong four times out of five and made money in the net. How do you know you will not get all the bad tips if you follow me and none of those that are right? You see what chances you are taking?

Unless your adviser follows up every trade until it is completed, you cannot fairly estimate the value of his brand of judgment.

Now that I have pointed out to you some of the dangers in this practice, do you not think it would be well for you to begin to *learn* something about the stock market?

Barron's Weekly Evaluates the Dow Theory

IN BARRON'S WEEKLY of April 24, 1933 we note this:

"If both the averages should succeed in breaking through, the Dow Theory would be saying that the market is in a major bull movement.

"It should be pointed out that the Dow Theory is not a method for getting into the market at the bottom and out at the top. Neither does it enable the speculator or investor to catch intermediate swings. It has been useful, however, in giving rather definite clues as to the major and intermediate swings of prices."

We congratulate *Barron's Weekly* upon such a frank admission.

Selecting the Best Opportunities

HOW is one to do this? Not by calculating the earnings of a company, for the manipulative factor may come in and destroy the value of all such estimates. Not by weighing "inside information," for the insider who is most bullish, is probably the largest holder. Nor do balance sheets and book values give you any idea as to how far up or down a stock is likely to move. The fact that you "like it best" is certainly no criterion.

The stock list on the Exchange is made up of some 1200 different issues. The most desirable things to know about them all, are: Which stock will move first? Which way and how far will it go?

In the study of ballistics, it is possible to estimate by two means the distance a projectile will travel when fired from a gun: (1) Exterior ballistics, in which the motion of the projectile is considered after it has received its initial impulse: when it is moving freely under the influence of gravity and the resistance of the air; then it can be calculated as to whether it will hit a certain object. (2) Interior ballistics, which require an analysis of the pressure generated by the gas resulting from the explosion of the powder; this is in order that the requisite charge of powder may be used to secure the initial velocity of the projectile without unduly straining the gun. These two methods combined, make possible fine calculations as to the distance a shell will travel.

When it comes to estimating the distance a stock will move in a certain direction, there is no such exact science, but an analogy is found in the fact that certain forces are generated before the stock begins to move, and that the distance it travels is the result of these, plus the additional forces which it gathers, and minus other forces which oppose it.

The accumulation of a stock on a large scale may be compared with the loading of a gun with powder. Absorption of the stock not only gathers it into one large holding but at the same time reduces the floating supply around the level where the accumulation takes place. The marking up period may be likened to the firing of the charge. The selling resistance encountered during and at the culmination of the rise, may be likened to the air-resistance and the force of gravity which tends to slow up the projectile before it hits the target.

In selecting the stock which promises to yield the greatest profit in the shortest time, we must therefore use some means of calculating the forces that generate the rise, or the decline. We must also estimate the probable resistance to be encountered as the stock starts on its indicated journey to its objective.

Anyone who has not made a deep study of this subject might say that such a task is futile — impossible of accomplishment; but for many years we have known *how* this may be done: by studying the *action* of a stock during its period of preparation for a substantial move. This enables one to sort out the issues likely to yield the greatest profit in the shortest time by putting them through certain tests that would be the equivalent, in ore dressing, to putting ore through a series of screens and treatments until finally the concentrate is completely separated from the rock.

We take a large number of stocks, say 100, and find that the majority are in a bullish position. This direction of the trend is confirmed by the further study we make of the averages and other barometers. In an up-trend we discard all groups and stocks that are in a bearish position because we must always trade in harmony with the trend of the whole market. Then we discard the individual stocks that promise to move only a limited number of points, for we prefer moves of 10 to 30 points. Naturally, those that promise 30 points are more to be favored than those that may afford only 10, and, as we are limiting our risk to 1, 2 or 3 points, the larger profit we get out of each trade, the better we are pleased, for it is percentage-of-profit-in-proportion-to-amount-risked that interests us.

By a technical method of calculating whether a stock is in a bullish, bearish or neutral position and *how far it should travel* when it starts, we are thus able to select the one, two, five or ten best opportunities at the moment.

Morgan Misjudged the Market

OTHERWISE why that $21,000,000 loss? But could anyone, no matter how expert a financier, how great a mathematician or how experienced in large security market operations, have foreseen the stock market situation for the two years following 1929?

Hardly that far ahead, but certainly the market foreshadowed its own downward course. Two months in advance it forecast the crash of November, '29, and about how far down prices should go. The market, by its own action, its fluctuations, its various technical aspects, supplied information obtainable nowhere else. The tape indicated more than even Morgan knew about it!

Why, then, study balance sheets, intrinsic values, earning power, dividend returns, business prospects, news items, and listen to gossip, rumors and tips about what is alleged to be coming, when you can obtain *from the very fluctuations* guidance of a character that surpasses in quality the combined judgment of the ten most eminent banking and business authorities?

How to lose profits in a bull market

Take the advice of "Experts."
Buy "graveyard" stocks — that do not move.
Get out with a few points profit.
Sell 'em short for a quick turn.
Spread your margin out too thin.
Be bearish because you have sold out.

Buying on Bad News

THE tendency of insiders to buy on bad news is well illustrated by the chart of American Tobacco B. This stock declined from 84 in October, to around 55 in December, 1932. For some weeks it ranged between 55 and 62. While it was around 57, December 3rd, there were rumors that the tobacco companies would reduce the wholesale price of cigarettes. S. Clay Williams, President of the R. J. Reynolds Co., denied on December 23rd that there were any such plans under consideration: "So far as the Reynolds Tobacco Company is concerned, there is no foundation for the rumor."

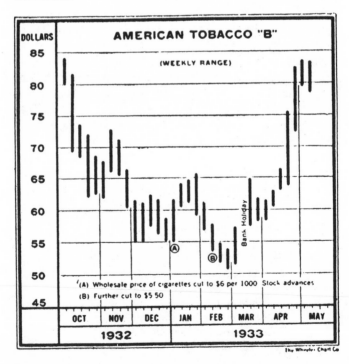

AMERICAN TOBACCO "B"

(WEEKLY RANGE)

(A) Wholesale price of cigarettes cut to $6 per 1000   Stock advances
(B) Further cut to $5.50

The Wheeler Chart Co

For the rest of the year American Tobacco B hung around 55 to 58 — a narrow range, but on a very fair volume, indicating activity under the surface — at the bottom of a 30 point decline.

On January 2nd American Tobacco and Reynolds announced a cut in the wholesale price of cigarettes from $6.85 to $6.00 per thousand. On this bad trade news the stock rallied 11 points to 66.

American Tobacco B then started to slide off. By February 11, with the stock around 54 again, the news tickers announced a further cut in wholesale prices to $5.50 per thousand. American Tobacco B, in the next two weeks, sagged off only 3 points to around 51; then it rose over 30 points.

It is a strange coincidence — not one that applies especially to the tobacco stocks, but to practically all stocks under manipulation: The bad news generally comes out at the bottom and the good news at the top of the swings. Take charts of many stocks and mark thereon the principal news items for any year and you will find that this generally is true.

The public usually buys on good news and sells on bad. Insiders and professionals do the opposite.

How About This?

What do you know today that you didn't know when you first started to trade in stocks?

Why do you believe you can beat the market now, when you have failed to do so thus far?

How much money have you put into the market in the last ten years?

What makes you think that with the $2,500 you have left, you can recover what you lost?

Can't you see that you have little or no chance of doing this unless you really learn how?

The Pool in Harriman Bank Stock

THE insider is often the worst judge of his own stock.

These Harriman bank directors, for example, who formed the pool and played the long side of the Bank's stock in a bear market: They doubtless knew the book value of the stock and the prospects for the institution better than any other group of individuals. Why did they fail to make money under these conditions? Because they ignored the Law of Supply and Demand, which is a better guide in judging the future price of a bank stock, or any other stock, than all the inside knowledge or all the values, no matter how great; or all the prospects, rosy or dubious.

When stockholders *wish to*, or *have to* liquidate their shares, they do not consult bank statements, or other statistics. Nor do they ask the bank's directors. Needing the money, or afraid of the future, they sell. What interests them is the bid price, not what the directors say or think about the bank's prospects. If the amount of stock they offer is greater than the bank pool of insiders is willing to buy, the price of that stock will decline. This is inevitable.

Bank directors and others should learn to follow the trend of the market for their own bank stock as it is expressed by the quotations. Unless they do that, they are in a much worse position than an outsider. Possession of inside knowledge, faith in the institution, confidence in its future, makes it difficult to form an unbiassed opinion. A person who cannot judge the market for a stock by its own action, without being handicapped by what he knows about it, is not justified in speculating in that stock, even though he be a bank director and a pool insider.

Will Rogers says: One hundred years ago there were no statistics. That was probably the worst invention anybody ever made.

Overheard in a Customers' Room

THE market had been reactionary for a week. Prices continued to decline until early Monday afternoon, when the tape indicated clearly that a reversal in trend was about to take place.

Customers' Man: "We just got a flash direct from the floor that the selling is better than the buying, and floor traders are expecting a big break."

Customer: "Close out all my long stocks and sell them short."

A canvass of several customers' men elicited the information that many customers had been hung up with stocks at top prices before the reaction of a week's duration had set in. Few had bought around the bottom Monday; but, as prices rose, toward Monday's close, they began to place buying orders.

Tuesday, prices rose consistently, from the opening to the closing gong. The room was packed; even standing room all taken.

Most of the customers had their eyes glued to the quotation board, or were spellbound by price changes announced by the caller at the ticker. Few paid attention to the volumes, excepting now and then some excited holder of a pet stock would shout triumphantly, "One thousand at a half: new high today." Or another proud owner of some inactive specialty, in which no one else was interested, would call out the price.

A distinguished, white-haired gentleman was pacing the floor with fingers in vest armholes, explaining half apologetically to anyone who would listen, that he had at last taken a two-point profit in Union Pacific. True, it was up six points more, but the "stock was new" to him, and he hadn't "quite got on to the hang of it."

I sought information as to what stock was best to buy at this time. Opinions seemed about evenly divided in favor of low-priced stocks, or those of "sound companies." With one exception, no one would venture to advise the purchase of any specific issue; he was very positive in his opinion: "Buy Ice!" Asked why, he informed me they had "gone into the laundry business, which everyone knows is very profitable." I refrained from reminding him that his "news" was over a year old. All other opinions were given with the precaution: "Just put 'em away a few years and forget 'em." Customers' men were meticulous in tacking on this self-insurance clause.

One self-important individual was imparting precious words of wisdom to a small, fascinated group. "Now this is inside information. He told me to watch the tape for a signal the pool would send out this P.M."

Such a superstition seems to be rather widely held. Just as though any manipulator would be fool enough to broadcast his true intentions by code over the tape! One follower of this cult exclaimed to me around 2:15: "There, did you see that?" "No," I confessed. "Well, it was the code signal to buy Steel. Now watch: it will close strong today." But though the close was down two points, the disciple's faith was unshaken. "Sometimes," he explained, "they give the wrong signal to throw people off." I asked if he made much money following the signal; but his reply was rather evasive. "You have to know just how to read the signals, and I haven't got on to the whole code yet."

A trader remarked that he had just heard from a friend who had cleaned up over $200,000 in the market during the past six months (and therefore ought to know what he was talking about), that the earnings of Con. Gas would be "off" and that the stock was ripe for a break of about ten points.

He asked me if I did not think he was right in considering the issue a good short sale. I suggested that he study the technical position of the stock, as indicated by supply and demand and let the *facts* tell him what to do, because it was barely possible that his friend might not have all the facts at hand. He agreed that this seemed reasonable.

While he was talking, the stock moved up two points.

Several customers 'phoned in for information. The customers' man's end of the conversation was: "It's all right; the pool has your stock well in hand and will put it up when the time is ripe — it may be next week, or next year. You just sit tight."

Is it any wonder the public loses money?

He who is silent is forgotten; he who abstains is taken at his word; he who does not advance falls back; he who stops is overwhelmed, distanced, crushed; he who ceases to grow greater becomes smaller; he who leaves off, gives up. A stationary condition is the beginning of the end. — *Amiel*.

A Letter to a Loser

My dear Friend:

The attitude with which the average successful business man approaches the stock market, is the greatest mystery to me.

Take your own case: From my acquaintance with you, it is easy to see that you are thoroughly and completely informed on the steel business, which you are in. You took a special university education to prepare yourself for "steel," learned it technically, chemically and every other way, although you were not going to manufacture but sell it. You have been careful in conducting the finances of your business. You are a shrewd employer of help; you have been careful in the renting of your office. Recently you described to me in minute detail how you manipulated your last lease so that you retained your present office at a substantially reduced rental. Your relations with your bank have been studied with extreme care and are of the highest order; I know this from what you have told me. You engage your employees after much investigation and are particularly careful to make close arrangements with them.

You have been successful. Hard work, skilled judgment, careful thought and close application to business have enabled you to accumulate money. This money, to say the least, is hard earned.

You have turned toward the stock market at various times in your life, and what have you done? You have placed thousands of dollars in the market and bought stocks on a basis of a few minutes' conversation with a customer's man in a brokerage office. When your judgment told you that you should sell, as it did in September, 1929, previous to your trip abroad, you went to your broker's office resolved to take your profits and get out of the market. But you let that same customer's man talk you out of it — reverse your decision.

When you returned from Europe a few months later, your losses had run into many thousands of dollars. When you thought you should salvage what there was left, you allowed your customer's man again to influence you, with the result that you did not accept your loss, but continued to hold until now your capital has been depleted to a fraction of what it was originally.

You conduct your business on your own judgment and with rare success. You would not permit one of your executives (who probably is far more able than the customer's man) to influence your judgment one iota; but in the stock market you throw away thousands of dollars — go directly against your own judgment — because a broker's employee tells you to do so.

Where is the logic, where is the sense, where is the judgment that is so much a part of your regular business? Why is it not applied to your operations in the stock market? Is $1,000 employed in the stock market of any less value? Does it deserve less care and consideration than $1,000 employed in your steel business? Are not both of these sums of money entitled to the same thought, care and consideration, when deciding upon your commitments?

I hope you really meant it when you said, "You make me feel like a damned fool — and that's just what I have been."

High Spots in a Wall St. Career

This condensed series is from Mr. Wyckoff's autobiography "Wall Street Ventures and Adventures Through 40 Years." It will be continued through nine more issues of this magazine.

1898   Steadily Advancing

UNION PACIFIC had just been reorganized and the common stock assessed $15 per share. Its price "3rd assessment paid" was around $17. Holders who paid these assessments were given preferred stock in the amount of the assessment, and this preferred, "when issued," was selling in the 40's. I wrote a memo to Price, calling attention to the remarkable opportunity seemingly afforded, with the probability that the preferred would eventually sell at par; thus the holder would get his assessment money back, leaving his common stock costing him $2 a share. Price thought well of the suggestion, and sent out many duplicates of it. These brought a number of orders to buy the stock. This bit of financial writing, published in this small way, was the forerunner of over twenty million pieces issued from my office during the following twenty years.

The manager of our Unlisted Security Department used to send Bill Gallagher around the Street to see what the other dealers wanted to buy or sell and to work up trade outside the telephone business, which he himself handled. Bill made frequent rounds of houses like Tobey & Kirk, Frederic H. Hatch, Gus Maas, H. I. Judson & Co. — a mere handful of people who eventually, in order to save so much running, formed the habit of meeting each other at certain hours under the big archway of the Mills Building, 15 Broad Street. Their number increased gradually. Dealers either came or sent clerks there. This was the beginning of the New York Curb Market, which is now the second largest stock exchange in this country. The New York Stock Exchange had had its origin in much the same way. Within a year, forty or fifty dealers and brokers were making a regular market on the Broad Street sidewalk. Later the market was moved out into the middle of the street, up toward the front of the Stock Exchange; then it moved down Broad Street just below Exchange Place. There it reached its greatest proportions as an outside market. Finally it was incorporated as the New York Curb Market and housed in its present building. As one of the founder members, I paid $1,500 for my seat.

A friend of mine who had been advised by his doctor to keep out doors as much as possible, bought a horse and a two-wheeled carriage. He took me out for a drive now and then. Thus one day he told me of an invention by a friend of his — a new horse collar, lined with a pneumatic tube and pumped up with air like a bicycle tire. Friends in Philadelphia had suggested that he form a company. I asked him if he wanted to make money in the manufacture of horse collars or out of the sale of the stock to the public. He said the Philadelphia crowd would probably make the decision. He didn't know a thing about incorporating or stocks, and very little about horse collars.

I gave him a few simple pointers on the financial details common to all such enterprises. One day a note from him said: "My Philadelphia crowd have decided to go ahead making horse collars and they have a factory in Philadelphia. They've also incorporated the company with a million one-dollar shares. You have given me some valuable suggestions and I have decided to send you the enclosed three hundred shares in your name. The stock is going to be listed in Philadelphia before long."

As most of my other "holdings" were one-share lots, and I was still on a moderate salary, this looked like quite a lot of stock to me. I sent this message over our private wire to our Philadelphia correspondent: "There will shortly be listed on your Exchange a stock named 'Pneumatic Horse Collar.' The minute it peeps, quote it."

Some days later I got this message: "Pneumatic Horse Collar $3\frac{1}{2}$

bid." I wired back: "Sell 300 at the market," and in a few minutes, for the first time in my life, I had $1,000!

The Syndicate was greatly disturbed that somebody should come in and poke their bid with even such a trifling quantity as three hundred shares; next day one of their representatives called and asked me to hold off further sales. He was eloquent on the company's glowing prospects. The Philadelphia Fire Department, it seemed, had adopted the collar; the stock would shortly be selling at $5 a share. I didn't tell them that 300 shares was all I had. I just listened. He said all the other holders were tied up in a pool and couldn't sell. So I started on a still hunt and succeeded in buying 1,000 or 1,500 shares. Immediately, I sold these in Philadelphia, netting a profit of $1,500 more. None of the other numerous deals I have made since, some yielding profits into the hundreds of thousands, have held as much interest as the acquisition of this $2,500 — my first capital.

Price's organizing and executive ability, combined with his tremendous physical and mental energy, gave him great capacity for work. He was inclined to spread out rapidly. With a bull market on and new wire connections and branch offices, we began to do too much business for the firm's capital. A new special partner was admitted: George Crocker, one of the sons of the famous early California millionaire. He brought $200,000 special capital and commanded considerable business. This enabled Price to take care of the firm's development.

I was personally benefiting by better positions and frequent increases in salary. Supervision of several branch offices was one of my new tasks. Another was cost accounting which allotted expenses directly to the branch office, correspondent, or department where they belonged, while wire rent and other common expenses were prorated. By working nights in addition to my regular duties I was able to give Price a statement which showed him just where he was making and losing money.

1899   On the Ground Floor

I would get to the office at nine o'clock in the morning. My lunch was sandwiches and coffee, eaten while at work. At six or seven o'clock we would have a square meal at the old Stevens House across the street. On our feet most of the day and working under terrific pressure, we were all fagged out; we felt justified in spending an hour over our evening meal. Then back we would go and work until eleven, twelve or one o'clock. For several months my average time of home-coming to my house in Flatbush was between twelve and two o'clock. It was an hour's trolley ride; I slept both ways most of the time. At nine A.M. I was on the job again.

At times we worked until three or four o'clock in the morning, then went to Dolan's on Park Row for beef and beans, then to the Astor House for a few hours' sleep. At the office again at nine. Sometimes Price came down after the theater and went to Dolan's with us. The other partners occasionally dropped in, at from eleven to twelve o'clock. They knew they could always find us there.

Our business grew larger than ever. Mr. Crocker bought the building at 74 Broadway, next door to our old location, and Price had it entirely remodeled for our office. I was in charge of the accounting department with 30 men. There were 125 employees in the whole organization by that time, counting those in the branch offices. The firm was recognized as one of the largest houses in the Street.

I felt certain that I would break down at this business, even though I did win increases of salary and more important positions. So I decided to leave Price, McCormick & Co. and to go into business for myself. When I told them this, they assured me that I was making a mistake. Soon after the new year Price called me in and announced that I would be given a small interest in the business if I would stay, and also power of attorney to sign checks jointly with H. H. Johnson. It looked like recognition and I said I would remain, although still nursing this bug about going into business for myself.

This was only two years and four months after I had joined them at $15 a week. I was just past twenty-five. The business had been more prosperous than ever during the past year. I kept the private ledger and knew that the net profits had amounted to about a million dollars, a lot of money in those days.

The year 1899 marked the birth of many important industrial combinations such as Allis-Chalmers, Amalgamated Copper, American Beet Sugar, American Car & Foundry, American Hide & Leather, American Smelting & Refining, American Woolen, Republic Iron & Steel, United Fruit and United States Cast Iron Pipe & Foundry. These companies represented consolidations of numerous scattered units in their respective fields.

The Amalgamated Copper deal was interesting. Thomas W. Lawson, financial mountebank, habitat Boston, was the confessed instigator of this operation. Originally offered at $100 per share, the low point in 1899 was well under par; then it rose to 130 in 1901. The panic of May 9 in that year saw it down to 60½. In the panic of 1903 the low point was 33⅝, around which figure Lawson always claimed that the stock which had been distributed to the public at three times that price was reaccumulated by the original distributors. This peculiar procedure has never been entirely confined to those having their headquarters at 26 Broadway.

1900   Floating Myself

Finally I did go into business for myself. I had already played my cards so as to be transferred into the Unlisted Security Department. There I had traded in securities over the counter and by telephone, and executed orders in the Curb Market. These activities were an excellent preparation for starting on my own account. Toward the end of the year I sent in my resignation, leased an office in the Empire Building, 71 Broadway, engaged a clerk and a boy, and at the end of the year moved in.

Starting with a few ten-share accounts and dealing in unlisted stocks and bonds, soon, by executing orders on the Curb and specializing in inactive securities, I began to make money. Within six weeks, Price phoned and asked if I had enough of being in business for myself. Wouldn't I like to come back? But although I had assumed an overhead of $7,000 a year on small capital I told him I was going to keep on flying my own kite.

Later in the year I signed a partnership agreement with B. J. Harrison and Frederic H. Smith, Jr. This was in October, 1900, during the Bryan-McKinley campaign and it was agreed that the papers would be destroyed if McKinley were not elected. The Bryan forces being completely routed, the firm of Harrison & Wyckoff began business on the day after election in November. I was managing partner. The firm did a gross business of $114,000 in the next fourteen months.

We were friendly with the firm of George P. Butler & Bro., who were handling Missouri Pacific and other Gould stocks for George J. Gould. Butler used our firm among others to conceal some of their operations. We thus earned commissions on fairly large blocks of stocks which we bought, or sold short, as per their orders. I could always tell when Missouri Pacific was being accumulated or distributed by the part we would be playing at the time; when we were picking up a few thousand shares at a time over several days, Gould was getting ready for an upward move. If Missouri Pacific suddenly rushed up ten or fifteen points and Harrison was sent into the Missouri Pacific crowd on the floor to bid loudly for ten thousand shares in one lot, the Butlers were selling through other brokers whatever volume the market would absorb, and the move was over. Harrison's bid would invariably be at the top eighth or within a fraction of it.

The trouble with the Gould forces was that they never varied their method. Manipulation calls for the deceiving of the public into doing the opposite of what the operator is doing; and after a game like the above has been worked a number of times floor traders, big operators and even the public learn to recognize symptoms of the turning points and play the same way as the manipulator. So after a while the Butler brothers didn't get the Gould business any more and we didn't get the Butler orders.

The firm of Ellingwood & Cunningham were good friends of ours. We did a lot of "give-up" and clearance business for them — five and ten thousand share lots of the active stocks. Many of these happened to be in the Morgan stocks and it was whispered about the Street that the new firm of Harrison & Wyckoff was a Morgan house. Of course, that didn't do us any harm. We had quite a lot of other manipulative business. Occasionally Harry Content, who was evidently handling Amalgamated Copper for the Standard Oil party, seemed to have instructions to keep this stock, say, between 90 and 93. When the price would decline to the lower figure, we would receive buying orders from him for round lots, and when it would advance to 93 or thereabouts, we would become heavy sellers.

[*To be continued*]

The only way in which one human being can properly attempt to influence another is by encouraging him to think for himself, instead of endeavoring to instil ready-made opinions into his head. — *Sir Leslie Stephen.*

Trading in Stocks as a Profession

Second Installment

OTHER fields in business or the professions are greatly overcrowded but not this one. There might be twenty million people in the market; their lack of knowledge, their technical errors, their misunderstandings, only make the way of the expert more easy. So it might be said there is no competition for the man who sets out to master the stock market.

Note the numerous advantages the trader has over the manufacturer. The latter must find a profitable field, invest capital in a plant or rent one, assume overhead, interest, taxes; undertake to meet a payroll, fight competition. He is in the boat and he must row. To shut down means heavy losses. He cannot close out everything at a moment's notice and stay out as long as he likes. The manufacturer is married to his commitments. Getting out of business, even temporarily, means a lot of complications. The merchant is in much the same boat. He must sign a lease, take on a staff of salesmen, advertise, study styles, judge markets, force the sale of unprofitable lines and all that.

Observe that the stock trader in buying and selling stocks goes through a number of the same motions as the manufacturer and the merchant. The trader studies the market situation, watches for opportunities, takes on the lines he believes will yield the greatest profits. He waits for a chance to liquidate these to advantage. With some he is very successful; others turn dead or run into a loss; he has them on hand and must finally sell them at a sacrifice. But he has no overhead, payroll or advertising expenses; all his operating costs are represented by the commissions and interest he pays his broker, and the taxes he pays the state and the government on his transactions.

The trader has another material advantage over the manufacturer and the distributor, in that he can derive profits from declining markets — as much, if not more than from advancing markets. The manufacturer with raw materials or unfinished goods on hand, or the merchant with his stock, must sell at a small profit or a loss when prices are shrinking. Not so with the trader. In a few seconds he can give an order to his broker: Close out all my long stocks at the market. And the thing is done. He has a clean sheet in no time at all. In the next few minutes he can put out a line of shorts so that he benefits by a reaction, a slump, a bear market or a panic. Thus it may be observed that a trader in stocks who understands his business, has a flexible mind, who is never tied either to the bull or the bear side, has a tremendous advantage over the merchant or manufacturer.

* * *

For nearly a century and a half the public has been playing the stock game in reverse — buying high and selling low; getting most heavily loaded at the top of bull markets, then liquidating and going broke in panics and depressions. Of what use, I often ask, is it to attempt to accumulate profits only to lose them again? A person who knows only the bull side of the market, who has no science, no judgment, no training or experience, is in most cases prone to do this. He is like the general who marched his soldiers up the hill and then marched them down again. He goes through all kinds of emotional strains, rolling up his paper profits, expanding his bank accounts, only to see these melt away because he did not know when to get out and how to ride stocks down.

The Street is full of people who make money in other lines of business and blow it in on the tape. Wall Street could not survive very long as a leading speculative center if the public did not dig up money from somewhere and continue betting on the quotations.

The whole atmosphere of Wall Street is alluring. But actually, to make a success there, you must really learn how to operate from more and more of a professional standpoint.

Perhaps some day every brokerage office may be required to exhibit at its entrance, a sign reading something like this:

> To trade in stocks and gain an ultimate profit is very difficult; most people do not succeed because they never learn how to trade. They think they are investing when they really are speculating.
>
> Speculation is a science. Do not plunge into it without any training. Unless you are willing to learn this business of trading in stocks, you had better put your money in the savings bank, in Government bonds; or buy annuities.
>
> Our customers' men will give you lots of tips and opinions. These may be good or bad. You can play them if you like; but don't let anything in their attitude or ours lead you to think that the stock market is an easy nut to crack.
>
> Of course you may make money at times, without knowing anything about speculation. It is not what you make, but what you keep that counts in the end.
>
> With that understanding we will accept your margin account and execute your orders for your account and risk; but you should not venture money you cannot afford to lose, and you must never claim that we did not warn you in advance of the dangers of speculation.

The public usually acts on herd psychology. They buy because everyone else is buying; because the market "is going up." When declines occur they become increasingly infected with the mob instinct which tells them everything is going to pot; so they feel impelled to sell while they can. After liquidating at low levels, they may perhaps even flop over to the short side.

Most people trade on their emotions, not their judgment. They fluctuate between their hopes and their fears, their ambitions, their cupidity, their timidity. Their egos refuse to accept a licking from the stock market. Usually they come back at it. It seems a reflection on their judgment.

One of the first things a person must learn if he is planning a successful career in stock trading is to limit his risk on every trade he makes. This is difficult to learn, but I might say that his success or failure as a trader will depend more upon the strict observance of this rule than upon any other one factor.

In a talk with Jesse L. Livermore some years ago he told me he had learned to trade in a bucket shop and that a great advantage lay in this sort of a beginning. The bucket shop, he explained, required him to put up two points margin and there was a certain protection in this. When he made a venture he did so knowing he had to get his profit before the stock went two points against him. Said Livermore: "I don't know what the Stock Exchange is going to do for big operators in the future. (At that time he was the most prominent.) Many of those who have been outstanding successes started as small traders and the principal thing they learned from the bucket shops was that they had to cut their losses short or be wiped out."

A friend of mine believed he could eventually make a success of trading in the markets. He saved $500 and began to practice in commodities. He made money, saw that he was on the right track; but he needed a lot more study and practice. Recognizing the risks in speculation and to fortify himself against calamity, he took up a profession so that he might make his living *in case*. He followed the profession and the market at the same time. Gradually he got to operating in a larger way; then he was able to give up his practice and devote all his time to trading. He went broke at times but he never was discouraged; always in some way he raised money for a fresh start. Finally he grew to be an important operator in commodities. These he understood best.

The stock market was a good deal of an enigma to him. He sometimes made money in stocks and eventually built up 50,000 share positions. On some days, getting in and out, he would trade in 100,000 shares.

Not long ago this man said to me: "I am through with the stock market. I've made and lost money in commodities and altogether I am way ahead on those markets. But I have lost seven million dollars in stocks and I am going to quit trading in them."

I asked him a few questions. First, "Do you ever limit your risk when you take a position in stocks? Do you ever use stop orders?" His reply was: "No, I've never used stop orders. I close out my positions when I think I am wrong but sometimes I don't close them out soon enough and often I have let big profits run into big losses."

Right there was the secret of his failure to beat the stock market up to that time. If he is to make money in this field he should, as Keene, Patton, Livermore, Cutten and ever so many of the other and lesser lights have advised, *cut his losses*.

As I once wrote: *Trading in stocks without scientifically limiting your risk is like wearing your pants without either a belt or suspenders.*

TO BE CONTINUED IN OUR NEXT ISSUE.

Statistical Guesswork

IN APRIL, 1921, a group of twenty-three bankers and economists sat around a dinner table. Someone thought it a good idea to ascertain how they all felt about the stock market. Every man proved to be bearish. All based their judgment and forecasts on banking and business conditions and statistics.

Within four months both the stock market and business conditions showed pronounced recoveries.

One of the economists who attended that dinner, who has delved deeply into the subject of forecasting from a statistical basis, remarked recently: "Forecasting by economic means, by the use of elaborate statistical data, is in my opinion nothing but making a series of what might be called mathematical guesses."

Judging Strength or Weakness by the Half Way Points

WE DO not subscribe to the theory that action and re-action are equal in the stock market because we have rarely found it to work out in a practical way. Even if it were true in the stock market, we do not see how one could make any money thereby. But there is advantage to be gained by watching the half-way points on rallies and reactions as a basis for judging strength or weakness.

When a stock advances two points and then reacts one point, it may be called a normal reaction; but if it reacts less than a point, it gives us an indication of strength. If it reacts more than a point, there is an indication of weakness. Used in this way, with the half-way point as a sort of measuring stick, we can really derive an advantage.

Other signs which may be included under this head are those extreme cases where, after a movement of say three points in a certain direction, a reverse movement takes place to the extent of all or nearly all of the preceding move. A stock advances because the buying power is greater than the selling power; but if it does not hold this advance: if it im-mediately reverses and loses all or most of what it has gained, this tells us that someone at once took advantage of the strength and sold the stock back to its starting point by offer-ing more shares than the buyers were willing to accept.

The same illustration may be applied to a drive down of say three points more or less, followed by a recovery of practically the same amount. This is a sign of strength: the rebound showed that there was more strength than weak-ness. This sign is more bullish than bearish because the sell-ers, having spent their force, are met and overcome by the buyers, who, at the moment of completion of the recovery, are in a comparatively strong position. They have taken all offerings on the way down and whatever stood in their way on the advance. The floating supply is thus reduced; unless further offerings appear higher up that they are not willing to take, the way is then open for a still further advance.

Study and learn all these technical points. Consider everything that appears on the tape as an evidence of support and lifting power, or pressure and selling power. Continually compare the strength of these forces. Use all the judgment and reasoning power at your command. Endeavor to improve your judgment by constant study and practice. Strive to lift your judgment from commonplace to good; from good to better; from better to excellent.

When your judgment has finally reached this point through your own efforts, remember that you can carry it to a still higher point by training your intuition; so that after a while you will get the pulse of the market and the psychological moment for trading down to such a fine point that you can form conclusions without conscious reasoning. You can learn to act on these intuitive conclusions and then go back and check up your reasons in order to find out how your intuition is developing.

What Partridge Really Said to Livermore

IN "Reminiscences of a Stock Operator" Jesse L. Livermore describes an old character designated in the book as Mr. Partridge, who used to frequent a certain brokerage office. Partridge never gave tips or advice; he never told how much money he was making. He did not trade actively. He was a good listener. But no one knew whether he ever acted on a tip.

Partridge always seemed to give the greatest consideration to the trend of the market and his stereotyped expression, when anyone asked him what to do about a certain trade, was: "Well, you know it's a bull market," which meant that he was going to hang on so long as the trend was upward; that the big money was not in the small fluctuations but in the main swings.

Livermore, after years of stock market vicissitudes, realized that this man Partridge had the right philosophy. And it was the influence of Partridge that induced Livermore so to change his plan of operating that his campaigns were increasingly successful for a period of years.

In a word, what Partridge said was this: "*It's my head that plans the moves but my backside gets me the money.*"

That is to say, old Partridge, when he once got his position, held on to it until the main trend had about run its course.

Most of the big stock market profits of operators of large calibre, have been made by following this same principle.

How We Made $35,000 from a Pot of Beans

IN WALL STREET one must keep his eyes open for opportunities. You can never tell when they are going to turn up. Every chance to make money is not first indicated on the ticker tape, as I found when I walked into one of a chain of restaurants some years ago.

I ordered lamb chops and was told they would take fifteen minutes. I couldn't wait that long. My eye caught an item on the menu: "Boston Baked Beans 40¢." So I said to the girl: "Start me off with those."

When she brought the beans I found there were seventeen of them by actual count, floating about saucily in a young potful of bean juice. Opportunity hit me in the eye right there. I said to myself: Any restaurant that can sell seventeen white beans for forty cents — two and one-half cents a bean — has a large margin of profit. I want some of that profit.

So I hunted up a friend who knew the proprietor, and I said: "Why not get that restaurateur to put his stock on the market? He's got a gold mine at the rate he sells his beans."

My friend nosed about, then told me a banking house was already planning the flotation; the stock would be offered shortly.

One morning coming down town I read the bankers' announcement. The stock was offered at something like $28 a share. From the subway station I hopped into a telephone booth and told my broker to apply for 1,000 shares. Soon he called back and reported they would only allot me 350 shares. "All right, buy 650 more at the market." The stock opened at a premium and he got the 650 so that the 1,000 shares averaged about 30.

The price advanced steadily. By the time I was ready to go to Europe that spring, it was selling at 45. I was not bullish; I expected while I was away there would be a chance to buy some cheap stocks. Knowing Bean Common was not a stock I would see quoted in the European papers, I sold it out at a profit of $15,000, along with some other holdings. When I returned to New York I found Bean had risen above 90. So my European trip, in addition to the fare, expenses and souvenirs, cost me $45,000 in possible profits.

That was years ago. The other day I was talking to the broker, and without mentioning Bean Common, he suddenly burst out with this: "Say, you remember that 350 shares of Bean you told me to get from the syndicate that year? Well, I thought if it was good enough for you I'd better take on some myself. I got 300 shares and I sold it at over 90. I made $20,000 on it."

Adding my $15,000 to his $20,000 profit, I find that my original investment of 40¢ in that pot of beans was not so bad.

100 Per Cent Judgment for the Long Pull

OF COURSE no one has such judgment, but we might stop a moment and think what it would mean. First, it would enable a man to know exactly when the bottom of a depression has been reached. He would then buy to his limit, on margin, all the stocks he could carry, at or close to bottom prices.

Next, he would be able to sell, on the big bulges in the market, the stocks that would have had, at the time, about all the rise they were entitled to. And with the funds thus released he would be able to buy, on the succeeding reaction, other stocks affording greater profits.

He would continue this process through the principal swings until, as the market approached the upper levels of the boom, he would gradually lighten his load. Then, at or near the top, he would clean house of all long stocks.

Meanwhile he would have been selecting and perhaps putting out, in the last several months of the rise, an increasing number of short stocks. He would not wait until the very top, because some stocks stop going up, then lie dead or begin to decline, long before the averages reach their apex.

His short line would thus be increasing while his long line was decreasing. When he sensed what he regarded as the absolute top, he would put out all the shorts he could.

As the market confirmed its tendency to decline, he might perhaps increase the number and quantity of his short stocks, selecting always those in the weakest position, not from a statistical but a technical standpoint.

By this procedure, through the years, he would benefit largely, whether the trend were up or down. With such infallible judgment he could start with a small amount of money and amass a great fortune.

There being no such person — who can trade without error — who can do exactly the right thing at the right time in every case, our description of him can serve only to show us how far from 100% our own individual judgment really is. It should also help to inspire us with a desire to improve the character of our judgment as far toward 100% as is humanly possible.

The Bargain Hunters

TWO outstanding shrewd buyers in the late depression, were Mellon and Loree.

In the 1929 boom, Mellon sold his common stocks and bought high grade bonds. In 1932, when prices were around their lows, Mellon was converting these investments into common stocks. Prices were way down. While we do not keep his books, we are confident his liquidation in the boom and his replacement in the depression will add hundreds of millions to his now staggering fortune.

Loree distinguished himself by capturing control of New York Central at an average price of something around $22 a share. Half a million shares went into Delaware & Hudson's treasury. Another half million were bought by allied interests. This buying began when New York Central was $10.

In 1870 N. Y. Central was an $8 dividend-payer. It never ceased to pay dividends until 1932, sixty-two years later. No one can dispute the fact that Mr. Loree secured the bargain of the century. He bought it steadily from 10 to 30. He could have saved money by taking more time, but as someone else might have had the same idea, he grabbed it while he could. Buying "at the market" was doubtless safest under the conditions. The effect on the future of Delaware & Hudson, as well as the strategic advantages now held by Loree, are indeed difficult to estimate.

These episodes teach us: In time of boom prepare for bargain day.

Odds Against Amateur Traders

PROFESSOR CARL N. SHUSTER, who holds the Chair in Mathematics at the State Teachers College, Trenton, N. J., stated, in a recent address at Columbia University, that the odds against the average man making any spectacular or permanent gains in stock speculation are greater than twelve to one.

We should say the odds are *twenty to one*.

Well informed Wall Street men are generally agreed that of those who enter the market without proper knowledge of speculative science, 95% lose their money.

Professor Shuster pointed out that the amateur speculator faced the keen competition of corporation officials, floor traders and specialists who could take advantage of the slightest fluctuations of the market.

"The best thing for the average man to do is to stay away from the stock market," Professor Shuster advised. "I know of very few amateurs who have made any spectacular profits or permanent gains from stock speculation. But if a man is going to play the market, there are certain rules he should follow."

Professor Shuster asserted that no amateur speculator should buy on margin, but if that was necessary, he should make his margin as large as possible, preferably 50 per cent or more. If the stock starts down and the margin is endangered he should sell some of the stock.

"Where the amateur speculator always fails is in taking his profits," he said. "There are no profits until the stocks are sold and the money is in the bank. The paper profits about which the amateur always talks cannot truly be classed as profits. The amateur fails as well in taking his losses. It is the expert who takes his losses gracefully before they become too large."

A STUDY IN TAPE READING

The chief temperamental distinction I think between a merchant and a speculator is that when a merchant has a small profit, his fingers itch to take it. All his trading inspires him to keep turning over his capital. Sometimes as I have observed merchants engaged in speculation, they have seemed to be most daring when they thought they were being cautious. — Arthur W. Cutten in *Sat. Eve. Post.*

Confession of an Investment Counsel

A FEW years ago, writes an Investment Counsel, I became convinced of the incompetence of the average human, so I determined to go into the business of advising other people how to trade in the stock market. Realizing that my own judgment was highly unsound and inaccurate, I devoted a considerable time to stock market research. I was endeavoring to work out a more or less cut and dried way of buying and selling stocks so that my hopes and fears would not destroy what judgment I had.

Considerable interest was aroused among my friends in my attempt to become an Investment Counsel. They felt that as I had spent over twenty years in mining iron ore I was fully qualified to forecast the stock market. I was, therefore, fortunate when after one year of research, one of them offered me a position in his brokerage office. My job was to advise other traders what to buy and sell — and when.

The business of hopping-them-in-and-out did not interfere much with my research work, for I did this after hours. What I hoped to develop was something like an annunicator such as they have for office boys: when the boy hears a bell and an indicator marked 3 appears, he knows just which desk to go to. I thought if I could get something like this — a sort of bell for the market to ring when it is time to buy something or sell it, I would be way ahead of these Investment Counsellors who have to figure everything out by statistics.

So I gathered all the ideas I could from all the other people who ever had anything to say about the market, for I was convinced that somewhere among all this (shall I call it mostly "junk"?) there was an open sesame which I could locate and apply in the solution of my problem.

Well, you know how much has been written about the stock market by people who know little or nothing about it, and you can imagine what a job I had sorting out all this stuff and testing these ideas, many of them lousy. But now that my years of research have been completed, and the results of operating according to my formula have been known to my friends for some months, I feel justified in announcing to a waiting world that I am ready to serve it.

Confidentially, I don't know any more about what the market is going to do than Jay Gould. And how in Hell does Jay Gould know?

I've had my people short of Manhattan Shirt since 1930. Under my guidance every Man Jack of them is an expert on a certain Theory. I have explained to them how conservative it is to wait several months to be sure that they get the signal before entering the market, and how important it is for any trader to jump in and out several times a day so his broker can pay expenses. Whenever I am in doubt as to the advantage of buying a stock, I protect myself by saying: "It is all right for a long pull." This, you understand, might mean anything.

Summing it all up, you can see that I am well started on my Wall Street career, and I have no doubt that those who follow me will succeed in losing not only all their money, but even more. Within ten years I hope to hold the record for having investment counselled more window jumpers than any other expert in the Street.

All I need to start is a loan of $10,000 capital and a straight inside tip on a stock that is a sure winner.

If you have knowledge, let others light their candles at it.

The victory of success is half won when one gains the habit of work.

We need the courage that is born of hope — and not only the will to believe, but the will to overcome as well — the determination not to be downed, whatever may happen. — *John G. Hibben.*

Advantages of Annuities

THE Annuity is one of the oldest types of investment. It was first mentioned in Rome about 45 B. C.

The possession of an Annuity gives you an income that is guaranteed for life — no matter how long you live.

For those who are along in years, it yields a larger return than is obtainable from any other form of safe security.

It is not dependent upon any one investment. It is backed by all the assets of the company issuing it. These assets are invested under State supervision and are widely diversified. You can further distribute your risk by buying Annuities in equal amounts from a number of the strongest companies.

A man 60 years of age can pay a certain sum into an insurance company and receive an income on this amount at the rate of approximately 9% per annum. If he does this at age 65, his income would be about $10\frac{1}{4}\%$. If he buys an Annuity at the age of 70, his income will be nearly $12\frac{1}{2}\%$. Where else can he get such a return — with safety?

The holder of an Annuity has no investments to bother with. He does not care whether stocks, bonds, real estate or government securities advance or decline; and his income is also free from Federal Tax for a considerable number of years. He receives his Annuity check monthly, quarterly or whenever he elects. All he has to do is to spend the money.

One man had an Annuity for every day in the year. Every morning on his breakfast table there was a check from one of his insurance companies, which showed him just how much money he could spend that day.

That is what I call real financial independence. I do not know of any other way in which a person's future income can be made so safe or so sure.

Certainly Wall Street can offer nothing to compare with Annuities.

RICHARD D. WYCKOFF

The Editor's Page

IN MANY writings on the Stock Market since 1907 I have frequently expressed this thought: Correct interpretation of the Stock Market requires a study of the *forces* which cause advances and declines in the prices of stocks.

These forces are constantly at work. They are of varying power, intensity and duration. They grow out of events, conditions and circumstances and acquire potency as a result of the acts of men, corporations and governments throughout the world. No one can anticipate the effect of these forces to the point of certainty, for no one knows when those now operating may be overpowered by greater forces.

These forces are accentuated in various ways. News items, tips, gossip play their part, but these are of limited effect until they cause men to buy or sell stocks on the Stock Exchange. No matter how bullish or bearish traders become, if their ideas and emotions are expressed only in words, hopes or fears, they have no effect upon the market prices of stocks; but the moment orders to buy or sell are given, functioning begins, and the effect of these orders is registered on the tape of the stock ticker.

The news may be bearish in the estimation of those who are selling; the bears may anticipate that their selling may make an impression on the market; but if at that moment there are other men or institutions whose brokers stand there with buying orders, ready to take whatever the sellers offer, then these sellers will have misjudged the probable effect of their sales.

How are we to know in advance why and to what extent someone else is prompted to buy or sell? We cannot know; it is impossible for us to foretell what actuates all of those whose orders are poured into the vast intake of the Stock Exchange machinery during the day's session. But if we study the action of prices; the responses; the speed of the

(*Please turn to page 27*)

High Spots
In a Wall Street Career

This condensed series is from Mr. Wyckoff's autobiography
"Wall Street Ventures and Adventures Through 40 Years."
It will be continued through eight more issues of this magazine.

1901   Inside Information

A CLOSE friend and a good client of mine was William O. Jones, Assistant Cashier of the Chase National Bank. We rode into town together every morning, and often home together after business hours. We would discuss the day's events and the market prospects. He had good sources of information. Every morning he dropped in to see Chas. H. Dow and Thos. F. Woodlock, of Dow, Jones & Co., and now and then James J. Hill, President of the Great Northern Railway, and other important financiers would come into the bank to see Mr. Cannon, the president. Hill called my friend, "Jonesy" and would often give him bits of information which Jones promptly noted in shorthand on a small scratchpad which he always carried in his vest pocket. This dope in turn came to me, and what I derived from it was of no small value to my clientele.

One morning, in the train, Jones said: "I was up at the Waldorf last night and met John W. Gates with some of his crowd. While we were talking about the market, Gates said to some one who had just joined the party: 'We're going to close our steel mills tomorrow morning.'

"Somebody said, 'What's the matter? Business falling off?'

"Gates answered, 'No, we're short of the stock.'"

The next day announcement was made that the mills had closed down. The stock broke from in the 60s to the 40s and 30s. Gates then covered his shorts, making a big clean-up; then he took a long position.

The mills went to work; the stock rose again. The closing of the mills had been nothing but a stock market maneuver.

One of the best bits of information that ever came through Jones was when J. P. Morgan and James J. Hill bought control of the Chicago, Burlington & Quincy Railroad. This purchase preceded an attempt to secure the dominating interest in the Chicago, Mil-

waukee & St. Paul. It was well known that the Morgan-Hill interests wanted a connection which would make Chicago rather than
St. Paul the eastern terminus of their system, and that they looked
upon the St. Paul road as the most desirable to this end.

My friend, Wilbur F. Herbert, was sitting in his office at 20
Broad Street one day, looking out of a window which gave an excellent view of the directors' room of the St. Paul, and of a meeting
being held there, when suddenly he became the witness of a very
animated scene. J. Pierpont Morgan had come to his feet; he was
standing, arguing, waving his arms, shaking his fists. "He wants
the St. Paul and he can't get it," my friend Herbert thought. Then
he saw "J. P.," evidently foiled in his purpose, storming out of the
room in a towering rage. The news slips announced that the St.
Paul directors had refused to make any deal.

Only a short time later Jones asked me to stop in at the Chase
National Bank on my way home and there he gave me facts and
data which indicated that Morgan, having failed to acquire the St.
Paul, had begun to buy control of the Chicago, Burlington &
Quincy in the open market in order to accomplish what he had
failed to do with the St. Paul.

Burlington was then selling at about 135. The original source of
the information was J. P. Morgan's office and Jones' data was unquestionable. Jones bought a lot of Burlington; I loaded my customers up with it. The stock rose steadily on heavy and increasing
transactions.

We knew from the same source that James R. Keene also had the
information; his buying wasn't hurting a bit. By the time the stock
got into the 160s those on the inside denied that there was anything
in the story. Many people knew what was going on but were afraid
to buy in the face of the advance that had already occurred. Knowing, as we did, that there might be as many more points profit in it
as had already been made, we held on, and bought more. Finally,
when insiders "admitted" that they had control, the stock was
around 195. We then cleaned up.

It is curious how skeptical men are toward real information from
the inside. They are stung so often by what sounds real that they
have no courage when the real thing comes along. There had been
a sixty-point rise in the stock, yet some people who got in early
had taken five or ten points profit when they should have pyra-

mided, and those who had held on for twenty points or more began to get dizzy and fearful. It is often said in Wall Street that "inside information will break anyone." Inside misinformation is what the saying means.

In those days I used to go to great lengths to find out what important people were doing. Not having many good connections, but making the most of those, I could have surprised certain large operators by producing memoranda of what they had done in the market during the day. For example, Charles M. Schwab was a tremendous buyer of Pennsylvania Railroad stock through a house on one of the lower floors of the Empire Building. I used to get a daily report of the number of shares he had bought on balance and my clients were long of Pennsylvania. I watched Schwab buy it up into the 160s and then suddenly stop. I've never known whether this was a stock market move in behalf of Mr. Carnegie or whether Mr. Schwab was employed by other interests to do the buying and see whether control could thus be obtained.

*　*　*

In the previous summer of 1900 rumors of great damage to the crops along the Northern Pacific had resulted in a decline of the stock to around 46. With the stock below 60 and on the way up, heavy accumulation now began to take place, although for no reason apparent at the time. Undoubtedly some of the largest operators were taking on a big line.

Then, through my friend Jones, I learned of important and continuous buying of Northern Pacific preferred. These purchases were distributed among various brokerage houses, but were traced to Kuhn, Loeb & Co. as the principals. At their office all of this stock would be finally delivered. Northern Pacific preferred was then selling below par, and as its dividends were limited to 4 per cent, there seemed to be no great advantage to anyone in buying large quantities of it at rising prices; there were other more attractive preferred stocks.

While the formation of United States Steel Corporation had stimulated speculation in every branch of the Stock Exchange list, the feature early in May was strength in railroad shares. Northern Pacific was one of the leaders.

On Monday, May 6, Chicago, Burlington & Quincy was selling at 198. Great Northern preferred was 188. Chicago, Milwaukee & St. Paul common, 185. Chicago & Northwestern, 206. Northern Pacific was strong on an increasing volume of trading, touching 110.

On Tuesday, the seventh, there was a boiling railroad stock market. Canadian Pacific was up 13 points — a great advance for those days. All the big rails and the little railroad pups were strong. But the transactions in Northern Pacific common overshadowed everything, amounting to over 400,000 shares, with the stock making 133 — an advance of 23 points from the previous day's high. There was a rumor that the preferred stock was to be retired; all sorts of stories sought to give the cause of the big transactions.

The market had a queer look. I didn't know what was going on but I could sense an approaching squall, and having made money for most of my clients on the bull side of the market, I now concluded it was time for everybody to take their profits and get long of cash. All that day and the next I was telephoning and wiring clients to get out and stand pat.

The morning of Wednesday, the eighth, was marked by what looked like heavy distribution in railroad and other stocks. But Northern Pacific was up to 149¾. Later in the day the rest of the market was clearly under liquidation and Northern Pacific still up; it was evidently cornered. Those who were short or had stock coming from abroad, or out of town, and who had to borrow the certificates, paid $700 for the use of one hundred shares of Northern Pacific overnight.

Came Thursday, May 9. The air was charged with excitement before the opening. No one knew what was going on under the surface of the Northern Pacific volcano. The chairman's mallet struck. Everything except Northern Pacific opened far down, and in the following hour, the nearest to hell I ever saw in Wall Street, the bottom seemed to drop out of everything.

Northern Pacific was jumping up fifty and a hundred points at a time until it sold at $700 a share regular way and $1,000 a share for cash. Those who were short bid $2,500, then $5,000, and finally, at one time, $6,600 premium was bid for the use of one hundred shares of Northern Pacific overnight.

Typical examples of the decline in standard stocks on that day follow:

Stock	Highest	Lowest	Last
Amalgamated Copper	116	90	106
Atchison	78¼	43	66¾
Baltimore & Ohio	102	84	94
Chesapeake & Ohio	47	29	41½
St. Paul	165½	134	141
Rock Island	158	125	146
Delaware & Hudson	165	105	150
Louisville & Nashville	103¼	76	95½
Manhattan Elevated	120	88	109
Missouri Pacific	103	72	93
Northern Pacific	{ 700 (reg.) } { 1000 (cash) }	170	325
Southern Pacific	49	29	45½
Union Pacific	113	76	90
U. S. Steel	47	24	40¼

This decline was the swiftest and most disastrous in the history of the New York Stock Exchange up to that time. A glance at the above figures — and this shrinkage occurred within the space of an hour — will enable one to realize that at these low figures not only were margins exhausted but many clients so deeply in debt to their brokers that the majority of the brokerage houses could not possibly have met their obligations if the market had stayed down at the low point. These were the days of ten-point margins. Disaster would have overwhelmed Wall Street had it not been for the rapid recovery that set in immediately after eleven o'clock. Within the next few hours the stocks that had been the weakest had recovered the greater part of their losses.

As the result of my warnings before the panic, most of my clients held now nothing but money; but in the gorgeous opportunity presented by the panic they failed to buy much at the bottom. In that hour of pandemonium the tape was so far behind that only through the report of executions and through telephone communications from the floor did we know anywhere near at what prices stocks were selling. But that was not the only reason. Most of my clients were scared to death. Two things must be possessed by people who buy stocks: money and courage. With the money and without the courage they all stood dazed and paralyzed. When the worst was over they were like men who had seen a cyclone pass; they didn't feel much like flying kites. After a while, however, they began to get back a little of their nerve and by twelve o'clock were scooping some of the remaining bargains. For the rest of the day I was busy placing their buying orders, and at the close they held substantial paper profits. These were subsequently greatly increased.

The panic demonstrated a number of interesting points about the stock market, the public and the brokerage business. First of all, it showed that no one can ever tell what is going to happen to the market nor how badly it will be affected by a single bit of news or a calamity such as this. Then it proved that, while real values are of most importance in the long run, much allowance must be made for the unknown and the incalculable. Not even the insiders who were running this fight for control of Northern Pacific realized, when they began, what harm it might do to millions of people who were operating in the market. But the conclusion I got out of it was this: That the action of the market itself was the best clue as to what it might do. The tape had said: Danger! That meant: Get out!

TO BE CONTINUED IN OUR NEXT NUMBER

A Talk with a Bridge Player

The Lady: I have been so impressed with your publication that I feel I can put my problem up to you and accept your decision. I have only a small amount of what was originally a substantial sum, on which I could live comfortably. First I invested my capital on the advice of my banker. The result was a heavy loss in money and confidence. I then went to a brokerage house and gave a customers' man authority to trade for me. He further reduced my capital. Much of what I had left had been invested in real estate mortgages. These also met disaster. I now feel that I must either learn how to invest or trade on my own judgment or put the balance of my capital in savings banks. Do you think it is possible for a woman without any experience, to learn to trade in the market?

Answer: I cannot make that decision for you, but I may aid you by asking the following questions: Do you play contract bridge? Are you a fair, average or better-than-average player?

The Lady: For a woman I am sure my friends consider me above the average.

Answer: In that case I believe you can learn to trade successfully. These are my reasons: To become a good bridge player you must first make a deep study of the game. The stock market is just another kind of game. You must have a clear head, exercise analytical powers, use good judgment, have an excellent memory and be able to execute your plays with growing efficiency. If you have not deceived yourself as to your qualifications as a bridge player, your chances for success in the stock market are excellent.

The Lady: Will not my lack of knowledge be a handicap?

Answer: No, in some respects you are better equipped than those who have their heads full of obsolete theories and impractical ideas. You must first make sure that you have secured a sound method of trading, one that has stood the test of time and then you can proceed to learn it without having to unlearn all these other things that are obstacles to the success of most people.

The Lady: Is there anyone in your organization that will help me in the study of this method?

Answer: Yes, and there will be no charge for it.

The Lady: How long will I have to be coached?

Answer: Just so long as you feel that it is necessary.

The Lady: How will I know when it is reasonably safe for me to begin trading?

Answer: When those in our Technical Department tell you, as a result of a series of paper trades, that you are prepared to begin actual trading.

The Lady: Will they tell me that?

Answer: They will do more: they will insist on your not making actual trades until they feel certain as is humanly possible, that you can enter the market without risk of taking substantial losses and with reasonable assurance that you can make your trading profitable.

The Lady: Suppose I find that I cannot trade successfully?

Answer: It would be worth far more than the price of the Course to know this; whereas, if you enter the market and test your ability by actual trading, the probability is that you will lose your entire capital. By studying the right method you are limiting your risk; you know exactly how much it will be — the actual cost of the method.

(*Continued from page 19*)

ticker, indicating urgency or the contrary; the intensity of the buying or selling, as indicated by the volumes; and the intervals when the volume is heavy or light — all these in their relation to each other — then we gain insight of the designs and the purposes of those who are dominant in the market situation for the time being.

All the varying phases of stock market technique may thus be studied and interpreted from the buying and selling waves as they appear on the tape. From these we form a conclusion as to the balance of the probabilities. On this we base our commitments.

The difference between the folk who do, and those who dream wistfully of what they will do, is not a difference of opportunity. It is a difference of spirit. The doers are fired with a determination that nothing can stagger; they are imbued with a faith that nothing can shake.—*Angelo Patri*.

An Amateur's Experiences in Wall Street

FOR many years I have been watching my friends dabble in the stock market. My income wouldn't permit me to trade, but I decided long ago that whenever I got a chance, I'd take a crack at it myself. So recently, when an uncle of mine bequeathed me a few thousand dollars, I thought I'd begin to investigate the possibilities.

First, I went to my banker. He wanted to sell me some Public Utility Bonds, but when I read that the government was going to sell power at Muscle Shoals for $1.50 a kilowatt, which is way below what other companies elsewhere are getting, I decided against those bonds.

Next, I subscribed to several Advisory Services. Few of them agreed with each other. Some were bullish, others bearish; some were weak-kneed and others just plain nutty. If I had followed all their advices, I'd be on both sides of the market at once. None were outstandingly good. I kept a record of their advices and found I would have lost money had I played them. I got a distinct impression that some were just playing to get my consent to *their* running my account, so that they could juggle it in their own way. Not for me. If anybody's going to lose my money, *I'm* going to lose it.

Then I took a number of financial publications and newspapers with financial pages and sections and tried to make something out of those. After delving deeply into all these had to offer, I began to wonder which stock I should buy or sell when loans were expanding and general business improving; when the dollar was going down; when more men were going back to work, but strikes were on; when wages were being raised and net profits probably decreasing.

The fellow who describes the chart movements in my

newspaper says that if the market doesn't break its old top, it might break its old bottom. I'd surely break mine if I followed his advice.

My evening newspaper says hogs have reached the top. Well, most hogs generally do. That seems no reason why I should either buy or sell hogs.

A member of the Cotton Exchange tells me that I ought to trade in cotton, because it is much easier than stocks. My evening newspaper proves he told the truth. It says: "Cotton was easier." But how could I make any money out of that information? Nothing is easy to a dub like me. It's all Greek. The more I get into it the more confused I am and the less I think these Wall Street fellows know about it.

I listened to a chap who talks to his subscribers on the radio. He told them they don't need a Service — they need a guardian. I decided not to take his letter.

I read that the monthly report of unfilled orders indicates that the Steel Corporation has enough on hand to last till about next Thursday noon; still, I don't like to sell it short, because the *Wall Street Journal* is printing a lot of bull stuff on Steel just now. This paper also says, in one of its circulars, "that Federal legislation is a dominant factor on the industrial and financial front and that through diversified reading I may be able to obtain a smattering of enacted and proposed legislation at Washington. Well, I don't see what good that will do me. I can't go long or short of Senatorial Preferred or Representative Common.

In the latter part of June, I got all primed to sell some stock short; but on my way to the broker's office to give my first order, I read a big ad from "the largest statistical and advisory organization in the World," which said, in big black type, "It is not too late to buy stocks for profit." "Well," I said to myself, "if they are the largest, they must know the most." So instead of going to my broker's I stopped at the druggist's and went long of a malted milk. Then I read that ad over again. It said: "Now is the time to act; for with recovery there will be profits aplenty for those who buy and hold the right securities." Of course I was foolish to think of selling short. That concern says it has over a thousand employees, including hundreds of highly trained specialists! Sure, I was crazy! But about a couple of weeks later, the market certainly crashed and I would have made money on my short sales. That didn't give me any more courage, because I saw that my itch to sell short was a good deal like a desire to lay a ten dollar bill on a certain race horse — only doing that, I knew I could only lose ten dollars.

My next move was to study all the opinions of the market letter-writers of the brokerage houses. I clipped these out, pasted them on cards, and sorted them into piles: bullish, bearish, neutral, confused, stalling. The bulls and bears about offset each other. Some writers seemed to favor both sides of the market. One said: "A drastic reaction can be regarded as nothing other than a remote possibility; so remote, in fact, that it could almost be classed as an impossibility. Nevertheless, it appears that lower prices will be recorded." Now, how was I going to make any money out of that? Maybe he meant I was to buy a hundred Steel and sell a hundred Steel at the same time and take a profit on whichever proved to be right. Perhaps you've heard of that way of trading; one old timer told me it used to be very popular. It is called the Will o' the Wisp Method.

I really think the brokers ought to compare notes when they write their letters; then they wouldn't contradict each other so often. A broker ought to know all about the market. Doesn't he watch it all day? And yet, I've found I can go to two brokers and three customers' men in the same office and get five different opinions. Why don't they work up a "house opinion" and everybody stick to it?

One broker writes: "Many floor traders express the opinion that the market wants to go up." Why not let it go up? I say. Another says: "Selected stocks should be bought on all dips." The question is: What is a dip? Is it a half-point, one point, three or five points? If I went to this broker and said: "Buy me a hundred Steel on the next dip," and it went down a point, would he buy it? I don't know. But if it went down three points and he had already bought on the one-point dip, I suppose he would explain: "Well, that was more of a dip than I expected."

Another broker says: "An elastic trading policy would appear warranted." Does he mean I should trade in rubber? Another says: "Reactions should be used to acquire selected stocks." Who is to do the selecting — I or the broker? I used to hear of a fellow who threw his chew of tobacco at the board and selected them that way. He sometimes won. How am I to know how to select them? What I am looking for is information. I am getting a whole haystack of it, but I fail to find the needle of profit. So far I haven't made a trade.

After months of such experiences I haven't found a man in Wall Street qualified to tell me what to buy or sell — and whether — and when; so I decided I knew less about it than I thought I did before my period of investigation. So I went up to my Savings Bank and said to the Teller: "Here, take this away from me quick, before somebody else gets it."

And I'm damned if I'll risk any of my money till I know something about the right way to play the market.

A Scotchman went to the Loan Window in his bank and asked for a loan of $10.

"All right," said the loan clerk. "Have you any collateral?"

The Scotchman handed over $25,000 worth of stocks and bonds.

"We don't need all this to secure such a small loan," remarked the clerk, pushing back the bundle.

Said Sandy: "Oh, that's all right, I might want to borrow some more. What rate of interest will I have to pay?"

"Six percent," was the reply.

Whereupon, the Scotchman turned to a friend and said: "Where else can I get a safe deposit box for sixty cents a year?"

Trading in Stocks as a Profession

Third Installment

NOW let us discuss the procedure followed by the author of "The Tale of a Bear" which appeared in the *Saturday Evening Post* of February 18, 1933; for anyone considering a stock market career should study the ways of both those who have succeeded and those who failed. "The Bear," after trading in stocks for over thirty years, stated that he knows little more than at the beginning, and most of that is negative. He stated further: Given causes cannot *ever* be counted upon to produce given results at a given time, if at all. Then he relates various instances which show how often his judgment and that of his friends — bankers, brokers and others — proved wrong. One must naturally deduce from his story that his successes were gained despite a judgment that was frequently unsound, because his predictions, expectations and commitments did not always work out satisfactorily; but when he did make money his profits exceeded his losses, else he could hardly have stayed in the game all those years. Or perhaps he had other sources of income.

He confessed that he had been caught in almost every collapse that occurred in his time; that his really large profits in the War period were wiped out in 1920 and later; that in 1921 he was broke: this after twenty years of trading. In 1928 he closed out his line about a year too soon, after consulting Raskob, Ayres, Reynolds and others. He missed the big money on the long side in the last year of the bull market culminating in 1929.

In February, 1929, he began to sell the market short — several months before the climax. In some cases he sold at bottom prices. When the market recovered he took in his short stocks at high prices and pocketed very large losses. This was early in May, 1929. In July he received conflicting opinions from capitalists and economists. The market meanwhile was leaping upward. Finally, on a mark-up of the rediscount rate, leading stocks dropped ten to thirty points and more. Our Bear again started to sell. Once more some of his sales were made at bottom prices. Then the market turned abruptly and was soon soaring once more, many issues making new high prices for all time. Again he covered his shorts at a loss that was uncomfortably large. Thus twice his fingers were badly burned by selling short at the bottom of a slump in a bull market. Finally, in September, 1929, he made his third and this time a successful venture.

I mention all these episodes in order to show how unstable was his judgment. He endeavored to analyze the market — the situation — by studying banking and business conditions and the usual fundamental statistics which are employed by most people in judging the market. He was influenced by the advice of friends.

To prove how unreliable was his method, I will give you a sharp contrast: A certain leading financial institution in London had carried a large amount of American stocks all the way upward in the bull market until September 1929. When that month was a third gone, the head of the institution called a meeting of the directors. His remarks were brief: "Gentlemen, the American bubble has burst. The New York stock market has made no upward progress for five weeks. I recommend that we liquidate all of our American stocks — at once." The directors agreed, and it was done.

Observe that our New York Bear had been wabbling in and out of the market until finally he got the right position and rode the market down, but the London bankers sat tight all the way up and were able to pick the psychological moment — the very top of the rise — for unloading. Why were these bankers able to do this when the Lone Bear was not? I'll tell you: It was because the bankers judged the future of the market *by its own action* and the Bear judged it by what *he thought* of the situation plus what *all his friends thought* of it. Many of the factors that helped him to make his decisions were already discounted in the market when he made his losing trades; but the London bankers, when they picked the top, were confident they were right because *the action of the market* had told them: This is the top and it is time to get out!

Note the further difference between their procedure and that of the Lone Bear: they did not run around and ask all their friends — bankers and others — what they thought of the market; they did not sell too soon and take a loss, then other losses and finally get in right. They got out at the right moment and not till then. They did not blow hot and cold on the market; they knew the game. It was clear to them what the market was going to do and they reaped a reward from their good judgment.

It is worth noting that few of our own great financiers, banking institutions, leading operators or investment trusts accomplished the same thing or anything like it. Here in New York where the Wall Street "interests" are supposed to know more about the stock market than anyone else, many of the big fellows went broke; quotations for most of the investment trust shares, run by them, evaporated. After the panic of October 29, 1929, the Lone Bear showed how wrong was the judgment of John D. Rockefeller, who announced that he was content with the decline and was buying stocks. I am told that another leading banker, in the first stage of the decline, bought stocks requiring the use of $100,000,000; these were carried in bank loans. But the decline continued, and later, he had to put up another $100,000,000 in cash, all of which must have been very annoying. So you see the biggest of them go wrong.

We must give the Lone Bear credit for having the courage and the good judgment to cover his short stocks at the first sign of a recovery from the low level of November, 1929, with profits enormous in relation to his commitments and in some cases much more than $50 to $100 a share. He had doubled his fortune as it stood when he first began to take the bear side nine months previously.

Next he was strongly urged to go long of stocks by men occupying high positions in American finance. He says they should have known better but they didn't.

Although Lone Bear did so well in the latter part of the bear market, I do not consider him in any sense an expert trader in stocks. No expert could be wrong so often and so badly. I call him fortunate. By this I do not mean that even the best of speculators can be right all of the time; a reasonable number of losing trades is part of the game.

My idea of an expert is a man who can spot the top or the bottom of the swings rather closely in the majority of instances. That does not mean taking a short position at the bottom of a slump which turns out to be a setback in an unfinished bull market. Nor does it mean covering at the top of a subsequent bulge and taking a considerable licking, for in most instances it is bad practice to sell on weakness and buy on strength.

In the next and concluding installment an
expert trader will be defined.

The Lord is on the side of the heaviest battalions. — *Addison Cammack.*

Speculation is the self-adjustment of society to the probable. — *Chief Justice Holmes.*

The forces that drive a stock upward gradually become exhausted. The stock hesitates, then stops, then begins to decline. Pressure increases until it is overcome by support from buyers. As these gradually gain dominance, the foundation for a recovery is laid.

The Trader's Prayer

O Lord, incline thine ear toward my troubles. You know how this market has been going down and down for weeks and weeks, and how I have been hanging on by my eyelids, and how my broker has beseeched me for margin from time to time. You, who are all-powerful, can certainly stop this decline if you only would; and I am sure if you realized how badly this market needs your support, you would do this — in a minute. Rally this market and send all of those bears to hell for taking the money out of the pockets of widows and orphans, not to mention your humble servant.

O Lord, of course I hope you will make an exception of Allied Chemical, of which, as you know, I have been short as a hedge. Don't rally that one, O Lord, for you well know that stock is selling far above what it is worth.

Let thy blessing rest upon my broker and all his customers' men, that their brand of information may be improved and their market opinions may be of far more value to me in the future than they have been in the past; especially that fellow Swift, who is always calling me up and jumping me out of some stock and making me buy some other. Bless him, O Lord, but make him give me a good tip *once* in a while.

And so spread your benign influence over all the rest of the world that the bear news will not be so bearish and things will improve for me and for all the rest of your servants.

Hear my prayer, O Lord, for I cannot hang on much longer.

AMEN.

Statistics Are History

THERE are three kinds of lies: Plain lies, damned lies and statistics.

Ours is probably the only office in Wall Street equipped with a stock ticker but without a statistical manual. With all due respect to our friends who publish these imposing volumes, we really have no use for them.

It is common Wall Street practice to investigate statements of earnings, balance sheets and other corporate figures as a basis for long commitments, investment or speculative; one seldom if ever examines such records as a basis for short sales. You might have looked up the position of New York Central in 1929 and found that its earnings were over $16 a share. It was an $8 dividend-payer. Its price range in that year was 256½ high and 160 low. Was there anything in the statistical manuals that forecasted a shrinkage in earnings to 49¢ per share two years later? Or that the price of the stock would decline to 8¾ in 1932? Assuredly not.

What you really want to know is *what earnings are going to be* in the months to come. You cannot find it in the manuals, but you can look for it on the tape. As Charles H. Dow said: "The price movements represent everything everybody knows, hopes, believes and anticipates."

Railroad, industrial and other corporate earnings are known to insiders way in advance. When you see accumulation in a certain stock, you may know that large interests are sufficiently impressed with its prospects to warrant their taking on large blocks of the stock. Such information is better than anything you can find in the manuals.

An investment in knowledge always pays the best interest.
Benjamin Franklin.

The Cascaret System of Trading

IN WALL STREET parlance, "Cascaret" is the name given to a system for playing the market. It is supposed to take the profits out of the fluctuations of a stock. It "works while you sleep," if the stock stays within a certain range. Little did my old friend Henry L. Kramer of Indiana expect when he originated this name for tummy-agitators, that Wall Street would apply the name in this way. Kramer made millions of dollars out of Cascarets as a remedy, then brought a couple of millions to Wall Street. There he would count that day lost when he did not trade in from one to two percent of the total volume on the Stock Exchange; but he never played the Cascaret System, so far as I know.

Of course you are interested in knowing about the System, but before we start, let me tell you that while some people have occasionally profited by it, I have found it in most cases a delusion and a snare; it kids you into thinking you are making money when mostly you are piling up some profits that are merely being loaned to you.

The System is this: If you have reason to believe that a stock will, for a long while, fluctuate within a range of 5 points—above and below say 50—that is, 45 to 55, without going out of that range, you start selling it short at 50 and every point up. Whenever any single lot shows a profit of $1\frac{1}{4}$ points, you cover it and put it out again on the same scale if it rallies. Should it decline below 50 you begin buying at 49 and each point down; whenever you can take $1\frac{1}{4}$ points profit on any lot you do so, and re-buy if the market permits.

This System would be perfectly all right if anyone would guarantee you against losses occasioned by the stock going above 55 or below 45; but should the stock go on up to 60 or 65, or down to 40 or 35, you are sunk, for it never may come down or go up to your range in the future. And if you continue selling on bulges above your trading range or buying below it, you may go broke.

On paper this is a marvellous system. I have known fortunes to be made in this way without wearing out a single lead pencil. It will actually work sometimes, in some stocks; but most of the time it will get you in so bad that you will regret ever having heard of Cascarets. It is an excellent system for producing commissions for brokers; but in giving your broker instructions, be sure to tell him that if the stock goes one point out of the specified range, either up or down, he is to close all open transactions at the market. Also in case you should, by any chance, cancel that part of the order, give him irrevocable instructions to hit you on the head with a club.

Stock Market Forces Compared with the Mechanical

IN THE study of forces that move the prices of stocks and in the investigation of mechanical forces, we find many interesting and instructive analogies. Such comparisons appeal to the scientifically trained mind and more particularly to members of the engineering profession. We find this one of the reasons why most engineers are fascinated by the study of the stock market.

The searcher for truth realizes, of course, that the study of supply and demand can never become an exact science, but to the investigative mind it soon demonstrates its right to be regarded as an approximate science.

The forces of supply and demand may be compared to the mechanical forces of pressure and tension.

One of the most interesting mechanical analogies is that of the testing machine. In this device, designed to test the strength of materials, a sample of metal, such as steel, in a form called a "test piece" is gripped between two powerful jaws; these are then gradually pulled apart by machinery designed for this purpose. The force of the pull is accurately measured throughout this process, until the "test piece" finally breaks. The force of the pull that caused the break is then recorded and the engineer makes the calculation to show the tensile strength of the material in pounds per square inch.

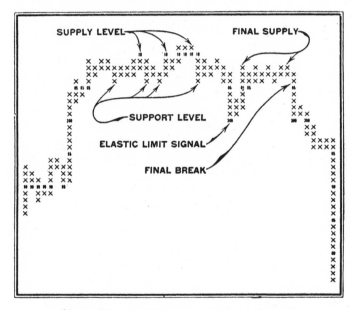

Chart of the actual price record of an active stock

During the progress of this test, and a little while before the final break, a very interesting phenomenon takes place. The measured tension, as indicated on the scale beam of the device, declines suddenly, conveying the impression that the "test piece" has broken. But it has not been broken; it has merely reached its elastic limit; it is beginning to stretch. Immediately thereafter it appears to show new strength, but this is soon followed by the actual break.

An almost perfect analogy is to be found in the behavior of an active stock which has been under persistent distribution for several days or weeks and is approaching the crisis which is to mark the beginning of a serious collapse. Serious students of market technique are thoroughly familiar with this development and make use of it repeatedly in their operations.

Study the Behavior of Stocks

"A BATTLE goes on in the Stock Market and the tape is your telescope. You can depend on it seven out of ten cases." — Livermore.

J. L. was referring to the habits and the behavior of stocks. As a board boy, at the age of fourteen, his job was to post up the changes in the quotations as they came out on the ticker tape. These interested him. He remembered how prices had acted in the past, just before they went up or down, and that in the advances and declines certain habits were indicated.

His keen memory for figures aided him in studying past performances of stocks and it was not long before he was anticipating the movements of prices. Reasons for the fluctuations did not concern him; he realized that the true reason for today's fluctuations might not be known for days, weeks or months.

By studying behavior one can anticipate not only the coming moves in certain stocks, but in the whole market, or any group of stocks. Behavior of the averages is different from that of any one of the big leaders. We must examine these characteristics.

Practically every move of importance is partially or completely foreshadowed by tape action before it begins; therefore we should study this action just as Livermore did. We must endeavor to discern the purpose behind the move, if it be part of a manipulative campaign; or in any case, study the technical forces that generate it.

Livermore's first trade was made on a tip. But before he acted on this tip he made sure that the behavior of Burlington justified his initial plunge in a bucket shop. This trade netted him a profit of $3.12. From this small beginning he gradually increased his operations until his line grew to hundreds of thousands of shares and his profits often mounted to many millions.

These same possibilities are open to everyone.

Flashes

A DOUBTFUL egg is nearly always a bad egg.

In the lexicon of stock market science there is no such word as tip.

The time to be most careful is when you have a handful of trumps.

Ignorance of the market is at the root of most of the losses that occur.

Why concern yourself with dividends? If you are on the wrong side of the market you can lose five years' dividends in five hours.

Sometimes it is scientific to go with the crowd; at other times it is scientific to go against the crowd. The main thing is to be right.

Reading all the financial news and evaluating it will avail you nothing. The market may rise on bad news and go down on good news. Then where are you?

A thorough understanding of the stock market will bring profits to those having little capital. Lack of understanding of the market has often wiped out millions of dollars.

A great psychologist recently said that the way to dope out the market is to analyze the mental make-up of all who play the market. But suppose he did that: It would not enable him to make money.

A trader who does not believe in selling short is like a motorist who insists on going along the left side of the street when the traffic rules clearly indicate "keep to the right." Sooner or later, in his wrong position, he will smash up.

A margin clerk in a leading broker's office said: "It is difficult to understand the basis of some people's stock trading. They seem to buy without any sound reasons and to be dominated by a desire to be in the market with the crowd."

Try and recall all the big losses you ever had. Then remember that every one of them — without exception — could have been avoided if you had been wise enough to accept a small loss when the stock went against you.

Why You Should Use Charts

IT IS foolish to keep charts if you can remember all the fluctuations in from five to fifty stocks for days, weeks and months back, with their opening and closing prices and the volume of trading every day for the period. But if you cannot remember all this, charts afford a great advantage.

The ticker records stock market history on a long strip of tape. The charts record the same history transposed into another form, more convenient, more valuable for the purpose of studying past performances as an aid in forecasting — I should say *invaluable.*

Why then, should those who are intelligent enough to use charts, be referred to as chart fiends or addicts? I'll tell you. It is because those who use such belittling terms are endeavoring to show their superiority over these chart persons, whereas it is the latter who are superior; they know the real value of charts.

So let the skeptics rave!

Buying Stocks on Weakness

LAST February, with a lot of banks in Chicago and other places beginning to blow up, I sensed a coming panicky situation and saw that it would afford a gorgeous opportunity to buy some cheap stocks.

Did I get out a lot of statistical books and look up earnings, dividends and prices? I did not. I simply took a copy of the *New York Times* and put a tick against thirty or forty stocks that were still paying dividends. It seemed to me that any company that could continue through the long depression without completely stopping its dividends was a good thing to buy, and so I chose the seasoned stocks that appeared to have excellent possibilities on the recovery.

After thus marking quite a lot of them, I began to weed them out and gradually boiled down the list to twenty that in my opinion were the most desirable, and sent it to New York saying I would let them know when to buy.

The situation grew worse. I waited until I thought the crash was about ready to come. Then I sent a wire to New York: "Now buy them." It was a night letter and the telegram arrived on the day the banks and the Stock Exchange all closed.

Well, I had missed that chance, so I had to wait for the market to open. Prices rallied and then declined. I began to pick up these stocks on the way down. By the time the market started up again, along about the first week in April, I had them all bought. It was the last decline.

At the top of the July swing these stocks showed about 50% profit. The dividends yielded an average of 9.3% on cost.

I didn't consult anybody. I wasn't guided by any advisory service, bank, bankers, broker, or customers' man. I just used common sense and some nerve. You must have nerve when you try to grab stocks while an earthquake is in progress.

Short Selling Principle Made Clear

MOST of those who dabble in stocks have no clear conception of short selling. Their ideas of it are distorted and fallacious.

Some people never think of selling short; others express fear at the thought of it; still others believe there is something unfair or even dishonest about it. These strange attitudes are of course due to lack of information, blind prejudice or failure to investigate.

People are quite willing to follow any impulse to *buy* a stock in the hope of profit, but it is especially the experience of brokers and advisory services to find that in undertaking a campaign on the *short* side of the market, their followers refuse to respond.

A prospective trader recently said: "Of course I expect to be in the market only about half the time unless there is a well-defined bullish trend, for I do not believe in selling short. I will only sell to secure a profit on long stocks when there are indications of a serious decline." Probably he never expected to sell anything at a loss.

We inquired: "Why are you so prejudiced against short selling? Don't you realize that most of the important businesses of the world are on the short side in their initial stages?"

"No, I do not. Please explain."

"You subscribe to a magazine. The publisher in accepting your subscription has agreed to sell you twelve monthly numbers of a periodical which does not exist. That is, he must collect the articles, buy the paper, ink, pay the printer and the postage and mail them to you. Until he has delivered the last number of your year's subscription he is short of that magazine."

"Give me another example."

"Suppose the buyer for a department store decides that several months from now it will require five thousand bolts of a certain kind of cloth in order to meet the demands of that season. He decides on designs, specifications, quantities and makes contracts covering prices and deliveries. The textile companies who accept the orders go short of that cloth. Their stock rooms do not contain the raw material. The cotton is not yet out of the ground and the sheep are running around with that wool on their backs. The manufacturers are short of that cloth until they deliver it to the buyer. This constitutes covering their shorts."

"I'm learning something about short selling now. Any more?"

"Ever seen a power plant under construction? The company that is building the plant undoubtedly has General Electric or Westinghouse short of its motors and other equipment. Some of the copper that will be used in the wiring and in the construction of the coils may still be in the refinery or even under ground. Surely that transaction is a short sale on the part of the big electrical companies."

"I now see the point clearly. The mere selling of a few shares of stock with the expectation of delivering at some future time is child's play compared with some of the really important short selling that goes on continuously in most lines of business. You have put me in an unprejudiced frame of mind. However, I have always felt that in a short sale the risk was very great because the sky would be the limit in case the trade went against me."

"I can meet that objection, too, but first let me tell you this: Trading on the short side has come in for a vast amount of discussion in the past year or two. Losers who were long of stocks in the big decline naturally blamed it on those vicious bears who were putting the market down. But as the New York Stock Exchange's reports on short selling proved, the short interest was never more than a mere fraction of the long interest and it was liquidation by the latter which pressed prices down. People rail against short sellers while continually selling short in their own lines. When they enter Wall Street they claim everyone should buy before he sells; that the trader who sells first and buys later is injuring the market for the stocks held by other people. They never give him credit for the fact that when he is short he is a potential buyer; that he *must* sooner or later cover his shorts, and that in so doing he is providing a certain element of support to the market.

Now as to the risk to which you referred: There is no more risk in a short trade than there is on the long side. In fact my experience has been that people lose more money on the long side than they do on the short. When they are short they are quickly scared and run to cover. But when they hold a stock, especially if it is paid for in full, they may hang on, as one English woman put it, for "yar after yar after yar." On the average, their losses on long trades will be ten times those on their shorts.

Besides, there is always a method of limiting your risk immediately upon making the trade; unless you learn how to do this correctly you will be very poorly equipped as a trader.

Remote Control in the Advisory Business

ONE feature with regard to the advisory business is that it seems to spring up in various locations far distant from New York. Ads offering sundry cures for lame duck brokerage accounts hail now and then from all quarters.

Originally, Old Doctor Babson held forth, from the woods and hills of Wellesley, that he had the New York Stock Market's horoscope down to an eyelash and would forthwith disclose, for a consideration, the market's past, present and future. Following the Old Doc's lead we have had no end of soothsaying ads from experts in Boston, Syracuse, Detroit and points north, east and west; in fact from such remote centers as Colorado and California.

No doubt John H. Trader (who wouldn't send a boy around to a Wall Street pilot with $10 for a month's dope) thinks "that guy way off there might know something." And who can tell? Perhaps he does — this month. Anyway, there must be something about these advertisements of our friends off in the sticks that coaxes the checks out of some bank books, or they couldn't keep going.

One naturally wonders whether distance lends ability as well as enchantment. Were we to follow the inference out to its logical conclusion, we would see clearly that those nearest the Stock Exchange must know the least about the market; floor traders, for example.

We have always been curious as to why these folks who are so sure they have a good brand of medicine, don't move in and settle themselves on the proper seat for operations of this sort.

With no special prejudice against the man who thinks that he is a better judge of the stock market when located way off in Kamchatka, Samoa or the Malay Peninsula, we are obliged to judge by gossip occasionally murmured on the village street that it wouldn't hurt their brand of judgment if they were to move a few hundred miles nearer Broadway. Such a change of base should not result in their knowing *less* about the market.

Analysis of Market Letters

WILLIAM DUNNIGAN of San Francisco is doing some very effective research work in matters relating to stock market procedure. In one of his reports he analyzed the advices of ten Advisory Services over the period from November, 1930, to March, 1933. Mr. Dunnigan says, "The recommendations of these ten Services are a matter of public record. They are down in black and white and cannot be disputed. Our conclusions as to the value of individual Services are based on complete records of seven Services:

(1) All seven have given unprofitable advice since November, 1930.

(2) An investor following all recommendations of the *best* of these seven Services, would have lost 40% of his capital.

(3) If he had followed the *poorest* of these seven he would have lost 63% of his capital.

(4) An investor who chose leading stocks at random, instead of following the advice of the *best* of the seven Services would have lost 48% of his capital, or only 8% more than if he had subscribed to the best Service.

(5) Had he chosen leading stocks at random instead of following the *poorest* of the seven, he would have lost 62% of his capital, or 1% less than the poorest of the seven.

(6) An investor who followed the advice of any of the other five Services (ranging between the poorest and the best) was better off than the investor who made random selections.

High Spots
In a Wall Street Career

This condensed series is from Mr. Wyckoff's autobiography "Wall Street Ventures and Adventures Through 40 Years." It will be continued through several more issues.

1902–3   Experiences in the Brokerage Business

AS A stock broker, my mind worked on three problems. First: How could I make money for my clients so that I could build up their accounts, retain their patronage, and make my own business successful? Statistics were my second concern: the study of statements, balance sheets of corporations listed on the New York Stock Exchange, so that I might become expert in judging values. Thirdly, I was bent on learning all about the operations of those who were big factors in the market — how they made their money, the details of their manipulative and pool operations.

Our firm was always on the lookout for real information on coming market moves. I was writing and mailing a daily letter on market conditions in which, also, I worked out the value of securities so as to bring them to the attention of our clients. My practice was to summarize the principal elements in the market situation on the day, and to point out one or two of the most attractive opportunities. We drew a good business from this letter. I constantly strove to perfect both the judgment of the writer and the character of the information. An assistant scouted the Street for news of what was going on among the real people and to get clews which might develop into good leads. All this was checked up from every angle. We were forecasting the action of market and selecting securities with a fair amount of success. This encouraged me to push on along this line.

Understanding of the action of the stock market demanded a form of reasoning entirely different from that applied to statistics and allied subjects. Forces were at work, influencing prices, which had no relation to real values. Many stocks were put up and hammered down by pools and by individuals for reasons of their own —

not because the value of these stocks was any more or any less. Understanding values was one thing; but the subject of manipulation, of the forces that artificially altered the course of prices through the various swings of the market, especially fascinated me.

Being on the lookout for panics and bargain days, I reached the conclusion that these came out of overextension of business, out of money situations, or they might have political or other causes. A panic was a psychological condition — a state of mind into which the public was stampeded, usually by sudden and unexpected events, or by a combination of influences which led to great uncertainty and ended in fright. (This was clearly illustrated in the panic of 1929.)

It appeared important that anyone operating in the market be on the watch for conditions that might lead to a panic. During a panic the market was at bottom, and usually there followed a year or two of advancing prices. While it was all right to be bullish much of the time, one must be guided by the record of the past, be ready to jump out when danger signals appeared, and then get long of cash in anticipation of coming bargains.

* * *

The great promotion and flotation period of the preceding years had ended with bankers, syndicates, pools and individuals loaded up with securities that had not been distributed. The public had bought its head off but had not been able to absorb all there was in the bankers' portfolios. The total capitalization of new companies had amounted to $8,000,000,000. Some had gone wrong. Morgan & Schwab's attempted consolidation of shipbuilding and steel companies had become wreckage. Confidence waned and died. Shares were liquidated through fear or necessity. The whole stock market was undergoing a terrific slump. Earnings of U. S. Steel for one quarter had amounted to only $2,000,000; 20,000 of the corporation's workmen were out of employment.

The decision in the Northern Securities case, by the United States Supreme Court, brought on a pessimistic attitude in the great financiers interested in railway consolidations. The downward movement was accelerated; liquidation of undigested securities continued; many syndicates closed out at a loss. Capitalists who were rich in certificates but heavily committed and short of cash were forced to let go wherever they could find a market.

The bear market continued for about a year. The Dow-Jones averages recorded a break in the twenty railroad stocks from the high record of 192 in 1902 to 89 in 1903; and in the twelve industrials from 67 to 42, indicating a shrinkage of about one-half and one-third, respectively.

*   *   *

As a natural consequence of its prominence and market leadership, United States Steel common stock had been the subject of one of the public's greatest speculative orgies. For a long period transactions had been 5 to 10 per cent of the total dealings on the New York Stock Exchange. More than once, blocks of 100,000 shares had been bought and sold in single transactions. The Steel Corporation's affairs were not only in the public eye but on the tip of the tongue of everyone interested in the market, in the United States, in Canada, in the financial centers of Europe.

When, therefore, the market for Steel Common began to weaken and its power to earn its dividends (then 4 per cent on the common and 7 per cent on the preferred) began to be doubted, the decline might as well have been the Chicago fire or the San Francisco earthquake so far as Wall Street followers were concerned. The very heart had been cut out of the market.

Pennsylvania dropped from 157⅝ to 110¾; New York Central from 156 to 112⅝; Chicago and Northwestern from 224½ to 153, and Union Pacific from 104⅝ to 65¾, but none of these carried the weight of influence to the same extent as Steel. The big corporation's securities continued to drop month after month, thus greatly intensifying the depression.

Morgan, when maligned for this decline in Steel stocks, said: "I was the company's midwife, not its wet nurse." When, in 1903, the price of the preferred stock had declined to 49¾ and the common was selling at $10 per share, I saw a letter which he had written in his own hand at the time Steel preferred was selling at par: "In reply to your inquiry," the letter said, "I believe that United States Steel Preferred at $100 per share is a sound investment."

And here was now the stock selling at $50! However, he had not said in the letter that the stock would not decline. Probably after creating this organization he did not know just what would happen to it.

1904   Up from the Lows

WITH Steel preferred at 50 and the common at 10, my partner and I took pads and pencils and began to do some figuring. At those low figures all of the common stock had a market value of only $50,830,000, and all of the preferred then outstanding of about $180,000,000 — $230,000,000 altogether, compared with a par value of $868,000,000.

We estimated that the decline in the stock market had wiped out much of the overcapitalization and that even though the preferred dividend were passed as rumor had it, the time was coming when the earning power would improve and payment of dividends be resumed.

The position of the Steel Corporation was unique. Taking the value of the sinking fund bonds, together with the preferred and common stock at the prevailing prices, the shrinkage amounted to about $450,000,000 in market valuation. The company, since organization, had put back into the property $200,000,000 in improvements, new plants and equipment. Its manufacturing costs had been greatly reduced and new economies were constantly being put in effect.

During the first year or two of its history it had earned the 4 per cent dividend on the common several times over. In the new period of prosperity which must inevitably come, it should be able to earn large dividends and make liberal payments to its stockholders. The corporation's big working capital, combined with its great earning power, should enable it to extend its operations without resorting to new security issues. Earnings in future years should be large.

Facts and probability said that the common stock should be bought for keeps. For when the dividend of 4 per cent would be resumed, the net interest on stock bought at $10 per share, the price now, would be at the rate of 40 per cent per annum.

We went into action right away. My partner took on quite a jag of the preferred and some common. I bought some common as low as 8⅝, within one quarter of a point of the lowest it has ever sold in the history of the corporation. When my certificates came in, I looked them over and said to myself: "Here is something to put away for my grandchildren."

But, I am sorry to say, I did not keep them that long. My grandchildren never saw them. Yet if I had waited for the World War, when the corporation was paying $17 per share per annum, I would have been making 200 per cent per annum on my investment.

Not long after we had bought, Steel began to creep up. There had been great activity in the preferred within the range of 50 to 60. Vast accumulation was apparently under way. John D. Rockefeller ordered a private telegraph wire run into his house at Tarrytown; the old man was soaking away bundles of Steel preferred in his safe deposit box — large as a bedroom — in one of the downtown vaults. The Morgans were buying heavily; they were telling their closest friends to get aboard again. The stock rose steadily.

Much of the inside buying took the form of an equal amount of preferred and common; that is, for each 10,000 shares of preferred, these large interests would buy 10,000 shares of common. At a price of 50 and 10, respectively, their investment was $60,000 per 1,000 shares of each, of which the preferred was paying 7 per cent. The net return on that combined investment was over 11 per cent. Later, when Steel common resumed its 4 per cent rate, the income from the two stocks was $11,000 per annum on the $60,000 investment, or over 18 per cent.

The general market, however, did not commence its upward march until June, 1904. There had been a period of a few months in which stocks had been held down within a narrow range, and the market was lifeless. This was the well-known period of convalescence which generally follows a sick market. Any tendency to advance was promptly knocked on the head because the inside manipulators' game was to keep prices still down while they accumulated. The result was a narrow whipsaw market in which traders, long or short, could not make any money.

These conditions make the public very bearish, for it is a well-known principle in manipulation that more people can be tired out and made disgusted with their holdings, and thus induced to sell on such a stagnant market than can be shaken out or scared out by a decline. In a steadily or swiftly declining market, many traders and investors will hold on, feed in margins and stick to their holdings in anticipation of a rally on which they can sell. Very often the rally does not come, or if it does, it does not go far enough. If it does go far enough, they will get bullish again, and hang on at the very time when they should be getting out.

My bearishness of the past two years had become habitual, for I couldn't see a thing that looked favorable. The event that finally woke me was the heavy oversubscription by the public of an offering of bonds by the City of New York.

The next day I went down to a little bungalow on the meadows behind Manhattan Beach, broke away from my friends there, jumped into a rowboat, pulled into a quiet creek where there were plenty of cat-tails, and said to myself: "If Moses first saw the light in the bulrushes, perhaps I may, too."

Lying in the bottom of the boat, staring at the sky and thinking hard, I gradually worked myself into an unprejudiced state of mind. I then sat up and jotted down the favorable and unfavorable factors in the situation. I discovered that there was a big balance on the bull side. It was perfectly clear to me that the market must immediately respond to the warning gun set off by the City bond issue.

The next thing to do was to select the stocks which offered the greatest possibility of an advance in what I regarded as the coming bull market. Here was an opportunity to make a shoestring grow into a pair of top boots.

[*Continued in the next issue*]

Answers to Inquirers

H. L. G.: The signature on the front cover of the financial publication you mention is not that of a person related to, or in any way connected with Richard D. Wyckoff. In 1926 Mr. Wyckoff resigned as Editor and became a bondholder in that corporation. At that time he retired from business owing to ill health, and thereafter did not personally conduct any advisory campaigns. A little later he disposed of all interest in his advisory business. He had nothing whatever to do with the advices issued by the concern that bought him out. Nor with those persons who illegally used his name in some questionable advices which were broadcast. Against the latter, his attorneys immediately took action. They were enjoined and barred from the mails. (For the facts in this case see the book, "High and Low Financiers" (pages 132 to 134) by Watson Washburn and Edmund S. DeLong, published by Bobbs-Merrill Company, $2.50.)

The Best Way to Buy Securities

IN ONE of the hotels where we stopped, the head waiter made this pat remark about the two dining rooms: "In this room we serve what you order, but in the other they eat what we give them."

People who buy securities from glib back-door salesmen are like those who dine *table d'hôte*. Those who select their own securities order *à la carte*.

The business of Wall Street is to manufacture and market securities. It is up to you to know what you are buying before you spend your money.

No such salesman ever admitted that he had a poor security. These go bad only after you have bought them.

Learn enough about securities to know a good investment when you see it without anybody telling you. That is to say, take your investments *à la carte*.

The best securities in the world are listed on the New York Stock Exchange.

If you buy a seasoned stock that has been dealt in on the Stock Exchange for many years, you are far better off than if you bit off a chunk of stock because the salesman's speel sounded alluring.

You can borrow money on your listed stock, or find a market for it at any hour of any Stock Exchange session. What the fake promoter sells you may have a market now — while he is boosting it — but this may fade out and finally disappear. Then what are you going to do with your certificate?

Most of the principal movements of the market are the result of operations by large interests who accumulate stocks in times of weakness, and liquidate in strong markets when other people are enthusiastically buying. These large operators act as a fly-wheel; their buying and selling tends to balance or steady what would otherwise be numerous highly erratic swings resulting from spasmodic buying and selling by the public.

The Law of Financial Success*

THE principles that will be herein explained have been found invaluable to those who are willing and capable of thinking deeply upon the causes of their financial successes or failures.

Any Law, to be really a Law, must rest upon the eternal foundations of Reality, and cannot be created, made or formed by the finite mind of man.

Is there, then, really a fundamental Law underlying that which we call Financial Success? Is there a Law which if once discovered, understood and practiced, will enable one to accomplish that for which this great modern world is so strenuously striving, toiling and desiring? Is there a Law, which, when operated, will make one the master of Financial Success, instead of a mere blind groper after its fruits? Is, indeed, Financial Success the result of the operations of a Law, instead of the operation of mere luck, chance, or accident?

Ah, yes, good friends, all this that you seek comes only from the application and operation of this great Law, which the successful men and women of the world make use of either consciously or unconsciously. And this great Law is as well defined as is any other Natural Law, and when grasped and understood may be practiced and operated just as may any of its related Laws on other planes of universal activity.

All progress, whether physical, mental, moral, spiritual or *financial*, is based upon Law. And he who wins success in any line does so because he has followed the Law or Laws pertaining to his business. Some of our great "Captains of Industry," who have won marvelous successes in financial affairs, have done so because they, consciously or unconsciously have discovered the underlying Law, and by concentrating

---

* These extracts from this book are presented by permission of the Regan Publishing Co., 26 E. Van Buren St., Chicago. Further installments will appear in succeeding issues.

upon it alone, to the exclusion of everything else in life, have manifested the operation of the Law to an almost abnormal degree.

Editorial

THE stock market is often referred to as a game, and I believe that to be a true term. Engaged in this game are the wealthiest and most powerful people in this country; their capital, business enterprise, foresight and ingenuity are employed in working out their side of this difficult problem.

It is not an easy game for the untrained outsider; it is almost impossible for most people to judge the future course of the market by the use of rules which ordinarily apply in other fields.

It is true that an experienced operator can so disguise his operations as to make them look like accumulation when he is really distributing, but he can only do this up to a certain point. There are ways in which his real purpose may readily be detected and a similar position assumed by a trader desiring to benefit by the skilled efforts of the larger operator.

True, the problem is one of interpretation. It requires training, experience and skill. Even the most powerful of those who operate in a large way are unaware of what the future holds for general business, for the stock market or for individual industries or securities; hence all such operations must be tentative, subject to correction or reversal at a moment's notice.

In their campaigns big stock speculators invariably assume a considerable percentage of risk. If this be true of the largest and most important operators, how much more is it true of those who trade in ten to one hundred shares?

Three may keep a secret, if two of them are dead.
       —Benjamin Franklin

Philosophy of Arthur W. Cutten

THERE would be no thrill in winning if you never lost.

Trading in too many stocks is confusing. It interferes with your judgment.

Most of my success has been due to my hanging on while my profits mounted. There is the big secret. Do with it what you will.

Each time you trade you are backing your opinion that the other fellow — the one who buys from or sells to you — is wrong. You reduce the odds against you when you consistently hang on when the market is running favorably.

Recent Books on the Stock Market

WHAT THE MARKET IS GOING TO DO. — Anonymous. (Robert O. Ballou, Publisher, New York.) $1.50

NO WONDER the author of this book has a retiring disposition. I have examined it carefully, even to the sales arguments on the jacket, and cannot for the life of me find out what the market is going to do. It merely contains an exposition of the reasoning employed when the author followed the policies indicated.

He says he made money from 1929 to the time he finished the book, and that what he has done, *any* man or woman of equal intelligence can do. How do we know how much intelligence he has?

Here is one of his bright remarks: (Page 88) "It should be the point of view to sell toward the top of the rise, unstable securities, anticipating a bear movement and reverse this policy toward the bottom of the cycle, anticipating a bull movement." Thus the reader knows just how to do the trick.

Then he gives a lot of indices (which anyone can procure by writing a postcard to most any advisory economist), and says: (Page 92) "I am not commenting on how to draw the conclusions from these indices, because presumably they are well-known to the organization of a corporate trustee." We wonder how that helps "the average man or woman."

Occasionally there *are* flashes of intelligence, like this: (Page 93) "I am also not commenting on what is probably of more value than an economic summarization based upon a knowledge of economic history, and this important thing is the ability to judge the technical condition of the security market from the standpoint of the indications as revealed by the action of the security markets themselves."

The average man or woman would have a fine time boiling this author's complicated formula down to a few rules that would be understandable and workable. We congratulate the author on having made money by the method he describes, but we defy anybody to do as well, or anything like it, on the strength of information derived from this book. One thing is certain: The title is a misnomer.

Baruch—A Most Successful Speculator

WHEN a certain big operator once said: "No man can beat the stock market," he was merely referring to his own limitations. For men — many of them — have, can and will continue to beat it; some more than others and more at some times than others, there being no more vivid or violently fluctuating career than that of a big operator in stocks.

For those who have been defeated, and for anyone who is skeptical as to the possibilities, we recommend a reading of the article on the life of Bernard M. Baruch in the October, 1933, issue of *Fortune Magazine*.

Starting his Wall Street career on a salary of $5 a week, he soon came in touch with a number of leading operators, such as M. S. Burrill and James R. Keene. Thirty years or more ago, Keene described Baruch as "the greatest speculator of his generation." Keene was undoubtedly right, for while many other big operators have flitted across the Wall Street screen, in and out of the limelight, Baruch has gone steadily forward, and today, at 63, confesses to a modest $20,000,000. That is not such a large amount, as multimillionaires were rated several years ago, but it is a whole lot of money for anyone to have kept through the panic and depression.

Here is a remark made about Baruch, thirty years ago, by a member of the Stock Exchange. My friend had just executed an order in a certain stock, and Baruch (a member of the Exchange from 1899 to 1917) also stood in the crowd. Said Baruch: "I recall that you bought that 500 shares of stock about ten days ago, and you paid so much for it — " (naming the exact price and fraction), illustrating his uncanny memory for stock transactions.

I remember in 1904 how the Guggenheims gave him free rein in handling American Smelting common on the Exchange. The stock had been lying dead in the 30s. He took it in hand and in the next few months whirled it up 40 or 50 points and made a tremendous killing.

The first thirteen years of his New York Stock membership are said to have netted him somewhere between $10,-000,000 and $15,000,000, made largely through a series of big deals such as on the short side in the 100 point decline in Amalgamated Copper from 130 in 1901 to a low of 33⅝ in 1903. Then he went into Goldfield Consolidated, Alaska Juneau and some sulphur mines, and from the latter into Texas Gulf Sulphur on the ground floor.

In 1917 he made his famous killing on the short side of Steel, admitting in his testimony before the Senate Investigating Committee a net profit of $476,000 on a maximum short position of 30,000 shares.

In the summer of 1931, it was reported to be his selling, said to be 300,000 to 400,000 shares, that started the market again on its downward course after making motions that indicated it might do better. Baruch had just returned from Germany where he saw the handwriting on the wall forecasting the financial plight of Germany and the probability of further extended liquidation. How much of that stock was long and how much short we cannot say, but the fact is he was right in selling whichever kind of stock it was. As he says, "I am a speculator and make no apologies for it. The word comes from the Latin *speculari*, — to observe. I observe."

After he sold his New York Stock Exchange membership, Baruch had an office uptown where he conducted his stock market operations so quietly that the Street seldom knew what he was doing. That he did not make money in every campaign is evidenced by his remark: "I have had some losses that would make an ordinary married man go out and shoot himself." Which merely proves the adage that no speculator can be always right.

The outstanding qualification of Baruch is his flexibility; he is not wedded to the long side of the market like most people. He has made big money on the short side at times. He can be equally as good a bear as a bull: Witness the past four years. Other Wall Street magnates with fortunes five to twenty times greater than Baruch's have been practically wiped out because they could not see calamity clearly indicated by the action of the market (to those who knew how to read it). They insisted on sticking to their guns. And the bear market converted their heavy artillery into little toy pistols.

There is, therefore, in Baruch's career a lesson to everyone interested in the stock market. His experience tells us that if we would be successful we must start at the bottom and build up in knowledge, practice and experience, increasing our commitments conservatively as we become more and more expert and looking upon the speculative field not as the arena wherein we make occasional plunges, perhaps with money that we cannot afford to lose; instead we must regard speculation as a serious business, undertaken deliberately with a profound determination to progress cautiously till we reach a point where we find our judgment becoming trustworthy. It is this procedure that has made Baruch an outstanding figure in Wall Street, just as Keene predicted he would be.

Bernard M. Baruch's career should be an inspiration to those who undertake to master the great game.

Trading in Stocks as a Profession

Final Installment

AN EXPERT trader is one who can recognize that the market is topping within a range of say two to five points. When he then takes his position it will be on the short side, not perhaps at the very top but on some of the bulges, perhaps the second or third after the high point has been recorded and the market shows cumulative signs of weakening.

When one knows how, he can detect the approach of the turning point sometimes one or two weeks in advance and when he finally takes his position he can do so, if he be a close student of the tape, with stop orders half a point to one point away from his selling price. In some cases stop orders of one-eighth or a quarter of a point can be used with a very considerable degree of safety. If you doubt this, ask any floor trader on the Stock Exchange.

It makes a big difference whether, in taking a long or short position, a trader is risking five or ten points in the hope of making twenty or thirty, or whether he is risking a fraction or one point with prospects of realizing the same profit. In the latter case his ratio of amount risked to possible profit is small indeed.

A large prospective profit in comparison with the size of the risk is the most desirable objective. This makes it clear why expert traders make money and why the public loses. Such a trader follows the rule expressed by the late Edward H. Harriman when he was a floor trader: "If you want to make money in stocks, kill your losses." This rule when followed by large operators has made big money for them, but all of their big losses may be traced to its violation. In departing from it they merely drifted back into the error to which the public is so constantly committed. As the experience of many former multimillionaires has shown, one might have combined resources equal to those of several of our largest banks and still lose every dollar by being overloaded, on the wrong side of the market, and letting losses run.

* * *

I define an expert operator as one who can make a large number of trades with only a few small losses. I have in mind two traders who, in the early months of 1933, acquired a knowledge of stock market science that enabled them to do things like this: In a series of over forty trades one man had three losses totalling 2⅝ points; his profits ran over twenty times his losses. Another, in the first three months of this year, in a series of trades on both the long and the short side of the market, made a few small losses but realized some thirty points profit for every one point loss. The record of these two traders sets a new standard in Wall Street batting averages.

The above instances merely prove that there are ways in which, by the elimination of losses and the application of intelligent stock market procedure, results can be obtained far in excess of those to be expected in most lines of business, in proportion to the amount of capital required.

To make a profession and a success of stock trading one must, no matter how much effort it requires, cultivate a sound judgment that will give him a high percentage of efficiency in his trading. Without this his successes are apt to be brief and unsatisfactory; his failures frequent and costly.

* * *

In the foregoing I have shown the possibilities in the field of Trading in Stocks as a profession; how it may be learned in spare time; why it is better to start with a small capital, and how, in a few months, a student can master the principles. Also why a large amount of capital is a handicap: it leads to unnecessary and unwarranted risks.

In becoming a professional trader in stocks one does not reasonably expect suddenly to emerge from a state of limited knowledge into one of high efficiency. He begins to study, masters the principles and gradually develops to a point

COMPARATIVE COST OF COURSES OF INSTRUCTION
IN VARIOUS PROFESSIONS OR GAINFUL AVOCATIONS

Cost of Course, in Thousands of Dollars
Average Duration of Instruction, in Years

0	1	2	3	4	5	
						Dentistry (a)
						Medicine (a)
						Accounting (a)
						Education (a)
						Fine Arts (a)
						Engineering (a)
						University (a)
						Retailing (a)
						Law (a)
						Transport Pilots (b)
						Business Administration (a)
						Commercial Pilots (b)
						STOCK MARKET SCIENCE
						Private Pilots (b)
						Mechanical Draughting
						Mechanics Course (b)
						Alexander Hamilton Institute
						Applied Arts — Student Classes
						Accounting and Business Law (c)
						Shorthand and Accounting (d)
						Secretarial Course (d)
						Shorthand or Bookkeeping and Accounting (d)

```
a  =  College Course (Average)
b  =  Flying School
c  =  School of Business Administration
d  =  Business School
```

where he can realize a net profit over losses, commissions, taxes and interest. The more he studies the more expert he becomes.

A distinct advantage of this profession is that it may be conducted without any overhead, employees or any other handicaps and impediments. One's time may be limited to a few hours a day, or all of his time may be devoted thereto. He may trade occasionally or continuously, as he likes; or he may stay out of the market for long periods, until opportunities develop which meet his requirements.

I do not know of any other profession which may be entered under such conditions: where there is no competition; wherein a trader may depend solely upon himself, control his own funds, and ask no one for advice.

* * *

With so many advantages one might naturally expect the profession of Trading in Stocks to be the most difficult, expensive, and to require a longer period of study than other professions. The opposite is true.

The graphic presentation herewith enables one to compare the length of the average educational period and the cost of tuition with other leading professions and vocations. It will be seen at a glance that the leading professions, such as dentistry, medicine, accounting, engineering, etc., require an average of four years' time to learn, compared with a fraction of a year for stock market science. Nearly all professions cost several times as much in dollars. No other profession offers opportunities equal to that of Trading in Stocks.

END OF THE SERIES

Have You a Bull Complex?

IF YOU have, by all means get rid of it. Under its control you are merely a half baked — a one-way trader. You are biased, therefore unqualified to form an opinion — uncolored by your leaning toward the Bull side.

A Bear Complex is bad enough, but a Bull Complex is much worse.

Most of the public are chronic Bulls. They nearly always buy first. They cannot see anything but "up" for the market. If you want to get them to buy, all you have to do is to advance the market and they will come in on the bulges. At the top of the market they have their heaviest load, and from there down to the bottom it is only a question of time until they are forced out, or tired out, or they get out because they are thoroughly disgusted with the stock market.

So if you must have a complex, make it a Bear. Bad as it is to be one sided, you might better be a biased Bear than a biased Bull. For if you are a good Bear you have the whole mass of the public working for you. The biggest and quickest money is on the Bear side.

But why favor either side? Why not be a Bull in a Bull Market and a Bear in a Bear Market and stay that way until there are sound reasons for a change in your attitude? If you say to yourself, "I can't sell them short," then you have no business to trade. Instead, become an investor if you like, and buy in panics and big slumps. But if you intend to be a trader, you must learn to operate on both sides fluently.

After all, what difference does it make whether you buy first or sell first? Your object is to derive a profit. So get rid of your complexes, if any, and ride 'em both ways.

Wiggin's Deal in B.M.T.

THE testimony before the Senate Committee that insiders sold out their B.M.T. before the dividend was passed told only a part of the story. Granted that it was true that insiders began selling on May 31, 1932, when the stock slumped something over 3 points to 26 and thereafter continued until June 8, when it touched the low of 11⅛, the action of the stock showed clearly when it was between 35 and 40 that a considerable decline was impending. We can hardly believe that none of the insiders knew or even suspected what was coming.

The accompanying chart shows the action of B.M.T. around its high point, 50, in March, 1932, and the decline during the three succeeding months. To anyone who knows how to interpret this, there was only once when the trend was in doubt and that was when the stock showed signs of a rally from 35. This rally halted at 40. The price soon returned to 35 and after recovering 4 points to 39 emphasized its probable downward course.

Looking at this chart, I claim that insiders sold a lot of stock above 45. Whether it was Mr. Wiggin or not, I have no means of telling, but supply overcame demand at that level. Demand just above 35 failed to persist, and if the chart says anything clearly it is that "somebody knew some-

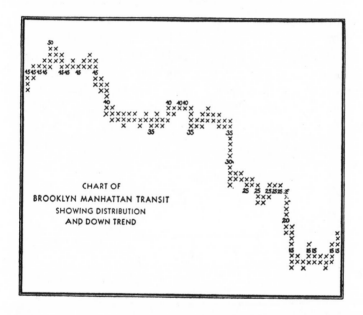

CHART OF
BROOKLYN MANHATTAN TRANSIT
SHOWING DISTRIBUTION
AND DOWN TREND

thing" and this was not bullish. So when we read that Mr. Wiggin, who was at the time Chairman of the Finance Committee of the B.M.T., did not sell until the first few days in June, when the stock ranged from 23 to 26, we are just a little skeptical. It hardly seems likely that the public knew more than the insiders and that all the apparently wise selling between 35 and 40 came from outsiders.

This episode is merely another indication that the tape tells the real story. Up to the time B.M.T. broke so badly you could undoubtedly have procured many bullish inside tips on the stock, but the ticker kept saying: Don't buy it. Sell it short.

Prize Contest Awards

O UR announcement stated that prizes would be awarded for articles of most benefit to our readers. Naturally those who have submitted manuscripts in this contest believed, in many cases, that they were complying with this stipulation whereas their stories merely recited some of their own experiences or those of others. For this reason a number of manuscripts had to be ruled out, although they were interesting and in some cases mildly suggestive as to correct stock market procedure.

The awards are as follows:

First Prize, $100, to Miss V. K.

Second Prize, $75, to Mr. T. L. B. of Fort Lee, N. Y.

Third Prize, $50, to Mr. J. M. Bateman, Cleveland, Ohio.

The following contestants deserve honorable mention: E. I. Brown, Mrs. Ruby Alinder, Barnard Powers, Edward Martin, Benjamin A. Huber, and H. C. Earle. Some of these manuscripts may be published later, and paid for at the announced rate.

Manuscripts which won the first and second prizes follow.

First Prize Story

I have been employed as secretary to an "Investment Counsellor" during the past six years. We handle many trading accounts, in some of which we have free rein to trade, and others in which our procedure is strictly limited by the wishes and restrictions of the client.

In most cases, as has been frequently pointed out to me, we can merely purchase stocks and wait for a rise, hoping to sell at a profit. We cannot accept small losses, because any suggestion that we liquidate a particular stock is resented by the client; to press the point may result in loss of the account. Frequently, this has happened. A small profit too often causes a cancellation of selling orders previously placed.

Rare is the owner of an account willing to accept an occasional loss. Rarer still is the trader who is not horrified at the thought of short selling, although our own experience seems to indicate that we can *almost invariably sell the market on a substantial bulge and replace our commitments more profitably later.*

We do have some real trading accounts, and the results obtained by such accounts make the standing long accounts look sick. With such clients, as have proven themselves cheerful losers, we are able to operate profitably even in the worst of markets. We find that the less profit we try to obtain from each individual trade, the better our chances of success. Further, we can make a half dozen trades which net a point or less against the single trade that nets three or more points.

Another rule that has been a sheet-anchor to windward through some terrific squalls in the market has been the "three and four day rule." This is the principle that the market rarely advances or declines in a single direction for more than three or four days. We have made many profitable trades on this rule. My boss says that he got this from some old issues of "The Ticker," published by Richard D. Wyckoff back in 1907 and 1908.

For active trading accounts we also use stops, and they are a great help in times of emergency. In July, 1933, we opened a few accounts in which, fortunately, we had full discretion. The first purchases were made right near the top of the market: We bought Steel at 62¾, G. M. at 32, K at 33-34, M at 27, B at 15 and other stocks at about the same level. Only stops saved us, for just about the time the whole market was ready to give way, X was bid up to above 67. This is an old trick, and would not have fooled us — we always are cautious when they start to mark Steel up in a big way. We were loaded heavily with Chrysler on many of these accounts, and, just as the market started to crumble, K made a new high at 39⅜. That warped the judgment of the "Investment Counsellor." It was fifteen to twenty minutes before he realized what was happening. Then he acted fast and his selling orders shot out. Even then much of our profit was gone before these orders were executed. In fact, in five or six minutes I believe some stocks dropped three to four points. Quick action did help us, and all of these accounts, even those opened only a few weeks before, were still on the profit side. But the accounts where stop loss orders had been entered were the only ones to retain anything like the bulk of the profits.

There is a lot more about the market that one picks up in my work, but I can only conclude by saying that we are always learning new things. Just about the time we feel we have learned the secret of its technique, something new occurs, and we have to vary our procedure once more.

Those who run this service eat and sleep "stock market." They ignore nothing — history, politics, finance, business; but principally they look to the market to tell its own story. They never fight its verdicts.

V. K.

The Third Prize Story will appear in our next issue.

Second Prize Story

In lower Broadway there is an office building which houses forty-odd members of the Stock Exchange who have board rooms where the public may sit to watch the ticker tape or translux. An acquaintance of mine has worked in this building for many years and has cultivated the friendship of one or more people in thirty of these board rooms. His method of trading in stocks is briefly this:

Daily he stops in for a short chat with each of his friends in these thirty offices. He ascertains his friends' opinions regarding the immediate outlook, and their current market positions, if any.

Approximately four hours after starting his tour my friend sits down in his own office and reviews the tabulated net results of his inquiries. On the majority of days the opinions are rather mixed; therefore his own market position is NEUTRAL. When seventy-five percent or more of his friends are bullish he takes a SHORT position in the market. Conversely, when seventy-five percent are bearish he takes a LONG position. Once entered into, a position is held (whether it be a matter of a day or two or a month) until the trend of his friends' opinions swing either to a neutral or an opposite position. Then and not till then does he change.

To operate by this method requires a man of genial disposition, who has a considerable number of friends that are very easy to reach, and from whom he is sure to get a real viewpoint. They do not suspect the manner and use to which he puts the information.

My friend makes money by operating in this way. He does not use judgment in the usual sense of the term. He coppers the judgment of the majority. And when most of them are on one side they are generally wrong. By taking the opposite side he is usually right.

T. L. B.

The Stockbroker and His Customer

Their Mutual Rights and Obligations

By JACOB SCHOLER *of the New York Bar*

THE panic of 1929 brought forcefully to the attention of brokers and customers many fundamental principles governing the relations between them which had not theretofore been fully appreciated. Failure to apply these principles resulted in numerous lawsuits involving substantial losses both to brokers and customers. In many instances these losses could have been averted had there been a more general knowledge and a proper application of the principles involved.

It is intended in this article to discuss briefly a few of the more important of these principles, also the questions which most frequently arise in their application, insofar as they relate to the purchase of securities on margin. These comprise by far the largest part of the dealings between broker and customer.

Although the customer pays to the broker only a part of the purchase price of the stock purchased — i.e., he has purchased it on margin — the broker must actually buy and pay in full for all such stock so purchased. True, he need not keep in his possession the actual securities purchased for his customer, so long as he has on hand, or under his control, the kind and number of shares purchased for the customer.

In the leading case in this State, and one which has been followed in practically every jurisdiction except Massachusetts (*Markham* v. *Jaudon*, 41 N. Y. 235), the law was established that the relationship between a broker and his customer is that of pledgor and pledgee. The relationship thus defined was based on the principle that the legal title to, and ownership of the stock purchased was in the customer, but that it was pledged with the broker as security for the payment of the customer's debit balance. The court gave the following excellent summary of the respective rights and obligations of the broker and his customer: The broker undertakes and agrees:

1. At once to buy for the customer the stocks indicated.

2. To advance all the money required for the purchase beyond that furnished by the customer.

3. To carry or hold such stocks for the benefit of the customer so long as margin is kept good, or until notice is given by either party that the transaction must be closed.

4. At all times to have in his name or under his control ready for delivery, the shares purchased, or an equal amount of other shares of the same stock.

5. To deliver such shares to the customer when required by him, upon the receipt of the advances and commissions accruing to the broker; or

6. To sell such shares upon the order of the customer upon payment of the like sum to him, and account to the customer for the proceeds of such sale.

The customer undertakes and agrees:

a. To pay or deposit the required margin on the current market value of the shares.

b. To keep good such margin according to the fluctuations of the market.

c. To take the shares purchased on his order whenever required by the broker, and to pay the difference between the percentage advanced by him and the amount paid therefor by the broker.

The principal obligation of the customer is the one set forth in subdivision b. Suppose the customer defaults in this obligation. What are the broker's rights?

The broker has no unconditional or unrestricted right to sell his customers' securities held in margin accounts. When he sells wrongfully — that is, without first having given the proper notice to his customer (assuming this requirement has not been waived) — the broker incurs a liability to his customer.

In the absence of any special agreement entered into between the broker and his customer, the broker has no right to sell such securities held by him for his customers unless he (a) gives a reasonable opportunity to his customer to keep his margin good, and (b) gives the customer legal notice of the time and place of sale, should the customer fail to respond to such demand for additional margin. While it has become the general practice for brokers to enter into special written agreements with their customers, it will hereafter be shown that these, unless carefully drawn and strictly adhered to, do not always afford protection to the broker.

The primary obligation of the customer, which is absolute, is to keep his account properly margined, an obligation which gives the broker the unquestioned right to call for more margin. Without such respective rights and obligations it would not be possible to carry on the purchase and sale of securities on margin. The entire structure of Stock Exchange transactions on margin is based on such rights and obligations. The customer who trades on margin should:

(a) Acquire full knowledge of the margin requirements of the firm with which he is trading.

(b) Be thoroughly familiar with the method of figuring margin requirements.

(c) Exercise as great care in not over-extending the credit in his account with his broker as he does in not overdrawing his credit balance at his bank.

The broker must comply strictly with the legal requirements when he desires to "sell out" his customer. He must either carefully exercise the rights given to him under any special agreement he may have with his customer, or else see that the proper notices are sent to the customer before he acts.

Nowhere must he exercise greater caution than in the form of the margin call and the sell-out notice. The margin call must be specific and certain and should state the amount of money or security demanded. After the call is made, the customer has a reasonable time within which to furnish the additional margin. What is a reasonable time depends upon the particular circumstances of each case, and is usually a question for the jury to decide. What constitutes a reasonable time is a variable factor; this must be evident from the fact that the requirements and conditions in times of panic are naturally not those which would govern normal market conditions. In times of panic and great stress, notice of one hour has been held sufficient. Under normal market conditions it would be advisable to give not less than two days notice.

In addition to the demand for margin call the broker must also give notice of the time and of the place of sale. In the aforesaid case of Markham v. Jaudon, 41 N. Y. 235, the court said:

"To authorize the defendants (brokers) to sell the stock purchased, they were bound first to call upon the plaintiff (the customer) to make good his margin; and, failing in that, he was entitled, secondly, to notice of the time and place where the stock would be sold; which time and place, thirdly, must be reasonable."

In fact, so strict is this rule that in one New York case (*Fairchild v. Flomerfelt*, 79 Misc. 42, 139 N. Y. Supp. 44), it was held that a notice stating that the stock would be sold on the New York Stock Exchange unless the margin were supplied *by* a certain hour, was defective for failure to state that *that* hour was the *time* of the sale.

The demand for margin and notice of sale must be made and given even in times of panicky conditions in the market, when there are sudden and violent fluctuations in price, unless under the terms of any special agreement with his customer the broker is authorized to and does sell without giving such notice.

In what manner must the notice of sale be given? Must the broker make a personal demand or give notice personally to a customer, if he desires to close out the customer's account? Contrary to the generally prevailing legal principles, mere proof of sending or mailing such a notice to the customer's address is insufficient.

The law appears to be settled in New York State at least, that a demand for additional collateral or margin and a notice of the time and place of sale, must as a general rule, and in the absence of special circumstances, actually reach a customer before the broker may sell out the account.

Even when the notice is sent by mail or telegraph, to the only address known to the broker, or in fact sent to the address *furnished by the customer* it is insufficient, unless the notice was actually received by the customer. It is not sufficient for the broker to show that he made efforts to give actual notice, no matter how diligent. That this requirement is harsh and even unreasonable is not open to serious question.

The broker, however, can protect himself by inserting a provision in the written agreement with his customer to the effect that the sending of notice by mail or telegraph to the customer's last known address, whether or not the notice is actually received, shall be deemed proper service of notice; and it is surprising to find that a number of forms in use do not contain such a provision.

[*To be Continued*]

Prospects for Anti-Stock Exchange Legislation

THREE questions are now agitating Wall Street: (1) Will the Stock Exchange be closed? (2) Will margin trading be abolished? (3) Will short selling be eliminated?

My answer to all three is No; for these reasons: The New York Stock Exchange will not be closed, because such a market place is an indispensable part of America's industrial and financial machinery. There must be one such place where buyers and sellers can meet; where the Law of Supply and Demand for securities can operate freely; where bonds and stocks may be bought or marketed and quotations established as a basis for loans.

No important civilized country in the world is without a stock exchange. This country positively could not get along without one. The United States Government benefits vastly by the established public market for its own securities that centers in the New York Stock Exchange. Would the United States be without such a market? Certainly not. Would over-the-counter markets serve as well? They would not.

But suppose, in these days of hasty legislation, some action should be taken against the Stock Exchange that would put it out of business — what then? Would trading in stocks cease? Most assuredly not. In 1914, when the World War broke out, the Stock Exchange was closed for over four months. Security trading did not cease. Those who wished to, or were obliged to buy or sell went to "The Gutter Market," which developed because people insisted on trading somewhere; and that is just what they would do if any ill-advised steps were taken to abolish buying and selling on the Stock Exchange.

The recent attempt of New York City to overtax transactions on the Exchange nearly drove the bulk of that business to New Jersey. Similarly, any attempt of this Government unreasonably to restrict or over-tax Stock Exchange transactions will result in all or part of the security market moving to Canada or to some other place where trading is unrestricted. If the Stock Exchange should be closed, New York brokers would do what Canadian brokers do now: they would send their orders to the place where they can be executed. Just as Canada now wires its orders in certain stocks to New York, so New York would then wire its orders to Canada.

As to the question: Will margin trading be abolished — my answer is that this would be practically impossible. You cannot make people stop doing what they wish to do, if they believe they have a right to do it. The Eighteenth Amendment proved that. If the Congress should declare to the American people that they shall not speculate in stocks on margin, the people will insist that they have a constitutional right so to do and that this shall not be taken away from them. Our government under the Constitution cannot deny its citizens the right to buy American stocks, or borrow on whatever property they own. Buying on margin is simply buying and borrowing. Laws that tend to restrict buying and borrowing will not eliminate speculation. People love to find ways to do what is forbidden.

Every man, woman and child possesses an inborn desire to take chances. The speculative urge is expressed in many ways. Laws preventing people from speculating in anything are bound to become dead letters. They always have; they always will. Americans will find forty ways around them.

As to the third question: Will short selling be eliminated? It will not — for very good reasons. It is 300 years since the Kingdom of Virginia enacted a law against forestalling, as short selling was then termed. But this has been going on ever since. Later in 1734, a Bill was passed in England penalizing short selling. It remained a dead letter for 126 years. It was repealed in 1860.

We once had such a law in this country. Advocates of government regulation would do well to read the report of the Committee appointed by Charles E. Hughes, then (1909) Governor of the State of New York, now Chief-Justice of the Supreme Court. This report was the outcome of public agitation against the Stock Exchange, following the panic of 1907. Panics generate these outbreaks from people who wire their Congressmen: "I bought stocks at the top of the boom and lost my money. Can't you do something to punish the New York Stock Exchange?"

The Hughes Committee reported that a law against short selling was passed in America in 1812 and repealed in 1858 by a Statute still in force (this was in 1909) reading as follows:

An agreement for the purchase, sale, transfer or delivery of a certificate or other evidence of debt, or any share or interest in the stock of any bank, corporation or joint stock association incorporated or organized under the laws of the United States, or of any State, is not void or voidable, because the vendor at the time of making such contract is not the owner or possessor of the certificate or certificates or other evidences of debt, share or interest.

The Committee went on to say:

It is the well-settled, common law in this country, as established by the decisions of the Supreme Court of the United States and of State Courts, that *all contracts* other than mere *wagering* contracts for the future purchase or sale of securities or commodities, are *valid*, whether the seller *is* or *is not*, at the time of *making* such contracts, the *owner* or *possessor* of the securities or commodities involved, in the absence of a Statute making such contracts illegal.

During the 46 years ending 1858, when short selling was illegal, short selling was in common practice, especially after railroad stocks came into vogue, as proven by the old-time campaigns in Erie and other stocks, by Daniel Drew.

But short selling will not be eliminated for another reason: Nearly every line of business involves short selling. The contractor binds himself to erect a skyscraper before he purchases a brick or a ton of steel; he has sold that building short. The manufacturer takes a short position when he agrees to deliver 5,000 yards of cloth before he has bought a bale of cotton. The department store sells short when it takes an order from a customer and says: We will have it shipped from the factory; such a short sale is covered when the factory receives the order.

Thus all through the American business fabric, short selling is such a *common* practice, so *indispensable* in the conduct of *nearly all* forms of business, that in order to stop it the United States Supreme Court must reverse its own decision, or a law be passed, the constitutionality of which would be open to serious question.

It is my belief, based on information from Washington, that no legislation will be enacted that will seriously affect the brokerage business or the public's operations in the stock market. From what I hear, there will be no legislation against short selling.

It is my belief that not Congress but the Committees of the New York Stock Exchange will do the regulating, when, where and as necessary. Margin requirements may be raised to 50% by a revised Exchange rule.

I believe, however, that there will be legislation against bank officials combining with insiders in large corporations; forming pools, manipulating stock prices and otherwise "stacking the cards" against the public. Also that there will be laws against officials of banks and corporations selling their own stocks short. Certain practices in pool operations may be curbed.

As to the efficacy of these remedies, there is much doubt. So many ways can be found to defeat legislation of this sort. How are you going to stop it, even though you admit that it should be terminated?

But whatever happens, nothing will interfere with the operation of the Law of Supply and Demand. This Law is all powerful — irresistible. It is even recorded in the Book of

Please turn to page 26

How to Lose Money in Wall Street

I. Buy High — Sell Low

IN THE popular Wall Street game of losing money quickly, Buying High and Selling Low is one of the easiest things to learn. To most people it is second nature; but, if you happen to be the rare exception, watch any chair warmer in the board room and you'll soon catch on.

Take your bespectacled neighbor, Jones; he looks so wise that you apologetically ask what he thinks of the market. Scanning you condescendingly over the rim of his glasses, he deigns to reply: "I'm waiting to see what they do." So you wait with him.

Around 2:30, the market suddenly becomes very active. The ticker vomits copious quotations for Can. The volume is tremendous. "Five thousand Can at 97¾!" shouts Jones. He leaps to the order window.

Hardly back in his seat, someone hands him a folded slip. He glances from this report to the translux, as 2,000 Can at 98½ glides furtively across its radiant face. Jones is beaming too; he shows you the slip. "Bought 100 Can at 98," it reads. "I liked the way it acted on the tape," explains Jones. "You see, I've already made my overhead!"

Ten minutes later some short-sighted traders must have taken profits on the day's substantial rise. Can closes 97⅜.

Next day, Can opens at 97⅜ and sags down to 95. Jones looks worried. "Doesn't act right on the tape," he mutters, and rushes in an order to close out "at the market." His hundred brought 94¾, the day's low. Slowly the price creeps upward, and Jones's pocket-book nerve itches to get in again. At five minutes before closing time

he can stand the strain no longer; he buys the stock back at
97¼, within an eighth of the day's high.

"I was a damned fool to get out in the first place," he
apologizes. "Next time they won't scare me that easy."

And they didn't. He must have carried it down to 89
the second day following; for it was selling at that price
around 2:50 when Jones was heard to grumble, upon re-
turning from the order window: "*Whipsawed again!*"

"Buy High — Sell Low" may sound at first like a lullaby;
but they sang it as a dirge at the obsequies over Jones's
bank roll.

Of course there are ways of reversing this sequence of
events, by buying low and selling high. But some of the
Joneses would rather lose money to the bitter end than admit anyone could tell them anything.

Ignorance may be bliss, but it sure is expensive.

II. Never Take a Loss

He happened to be my seat partner on a train speeding
out of New York one afternoon. I never saw him before,
but a glance over my shoulder while I scanned the day's
stock prices evidently afforded the excuse for a conversation.

"Ever dabble in stocks?" he ventured. Then, without
waiting for a reply: "Hard game these days, with all the sur-
prises sprung from Washington. They used to catch me in
those traps; but never again. I've learned my lesson."

I laid my paper aside. "How so?"

"Well, it happened this way: One day, early in January,
I was going over a bunch of monthly statements, when it
struck me all of a sudden that there had been *scarcely one* of
all the trades I had closed out at a loss that year which would
not have shown a profit eventually — if I'd only held on
long enough. So I says to myself: 'Jim, old man, you're
turning over a new leaf. Hereafter, if a stock goes against
you, you're going to hold on until it comes back and shows

a profit.' Since that day I've made it an invariable rule never to take a loss."

"When did you make that resolution?" I inquired.

"It was on the first day of January, 1929."

"And how has it panned out? Are you ahead?"

"Well, not right now. You see I bought some high-priced stuff in the autumn of 1929. But I held on. Bought more on the way down, to average. Kept putting up more and more margin until last summer, when I bought the whole lot outright. It all averages me about fifty points above present quotations and, if the market keeps on rising, I'll have a profit within a year or two."

"So your trading operations over the past four years really show a loss?"

The stranger turned upon me with a show of resentment: "Oh no. That's only a *paper* loss. I *never* take a loss."

"I knew a man," said I, "who got in wrong on the eve

of that crash; but he promptly took a three-point loss, and then went short for a thirty-point profit."

"Excuse me, sir," he ejaculated; "but this is the place where I get off."

III. When You See a Profit, Grab It

Probably I shall not meet that stranger again after his stocks come back to the average price he paid. If they were of the Middle West Utilities variety, of course they never will come back. But it's a gold dollar to one of the inflation kind that, if they do come back, he'll grab a point profit on any lot when he sees it, and justify himself with the wise crack:

"You'll never grow poor taking profits."

If taking a one-point profit in five or six years is a way to keep out of the poorhouse, why not sell apples on the street corner? It ties up less capital.

Continued from page 22

Genesis that a certain buyer, Esau, kept bidding higher and higher for a mess of pottage until he finally bid his birthright. His brother Jacob filled the bid.

Nothing interferes with the operation of this law; and it will continue to govern prices in spite of Government or other attempts to regulate it. It is self-adjusting to the many factors that influence the market and no legislation in the world has ever more than temporarily interfered with it. It is the one Fundamental Factor.

While no one can predict with 100% accuracy just what will come out of Washington in the next few months, these are the indications at the present time. And there is nothing in the legislative outlook that need disturb the average trader or investor.

Little Visits to Big Plants

I. General Electric

ARENDT VAN CURLER discovered Schenectady, meaning in the Mohawk language "The sandy plains beyond Albany," in 1661. Thomas A. Edison discovered it in 1886. With true Dutch liberality Van Curler paid the Indians "600 hands, good white wampum, 6 coates duffels, 30 bbls lead, 6 bagges powder" for their lands. Repenting of the bargain, the Indians, twenty-nine years later, aided by their French allies, burned the infant settlement and slaughtered all within its walls, wiping the town off the local map.

Edison did better. He put Schenectady on the World Map. When he bought two low, red-brick buildings in the swampy western part of the town, he founded the world's greatest electrical manufacturing industry. Far-seeing townsfolk contributed $35,000 to help Edison start manufacturing his new-fangled incandescent lamp. Never did an investment repay a community more handsomely. General Electric's employees and families now make up nearly a third of Schenectady's 100,000 and in good times the company's payroll is approximately $1,000,000 a week.

The two buildings Edison bought are still in use. On No. 10 is a bronze tablet in memory of America's greatest inventor and his founding this vast electrical workshop.

The Schenectady plant is but one of 21 owned and operated by General Electric. It was selected for this particular visit not only because of its size and historical interest, but because it is known as the "Mother Plant." Here is located the famous "House of Magic" where over 300 scientists are engaged in experimentation and research. Every year General Electric spends thus $1,500,000 to $2,000,000. Results periodically startle the scientific world. For example, the present incandescent lamp, which is nearly a thousand times more efficient than Edison's original product, is one result of laboratory research.

In Schenectady large-scale experiments are conducted. To demonstrate and test out the mercury-vapor boiler (invention of W. L. R. Emmet, one of the scientists), the company has built a complete power plant equipped with mercury-vapor boilers, at a cost of $4,000,000. In these boilers mercury vapor is used in place of water. Result: large savings in fuel costs, estimated at 30%.

In the Reception House, near the main gate, your credentials are examined and your pass issued, while from an oil painting the wizard Steinmetz, who never drew a fixed salary or wore an overcoat, looks down. Guides conduct daily, three tours of the plant for the general public, who approximate 50,000 each year. Armed as an ambassador of STOCK MARKET TECHNIQUE, with letters to those in high places, my blue check passed me through. It specified where I was to go; but as I was personally conducted by the General Superintendent, I fear I broke at least one rule laid down for visiting firemen and such.

Inside the gates I found myself on a wide asphalted avenue lined on either side with squat buildings extending almost as far as eye could reach. My first impression was one of quietness, then of orderliness and then of businesslikeness, if there be such a word. I had expected to be swept along among throngs of hurrying workers, my ears deafened by whistles and the clang of mighty machines. Such there were in plenty, but for the most part they are silent monsters. As for sounds, I might have been in Wall Street of a Sunday morning. It was hard to believe that more than 9000 men were toiling that day.

Here are a few figures on the size of the plant: Schenectady holds one-third of General Electric's productive capacity. Its principal products are: Steam turbines, large alternating and direct current generators, high power cable, large synchronous motors, porcelain used in electrical equipment, large synchronous converters, wire, large motor generator sets, induction motors, photoelectric cells, industrial control equipment, voltage regulators, electric refrigerators, synchronous condensers, water power and generating apparatus, radio transmitters, mercury-arc rectifiers, marine and aircraft equipment, air conditioning equipment, oil furnaces, laminated products, varnish and japan, carbon brushes, plastics (moulded insulation).

Normally 20,000 persons are employed; 1929 record, 27,000. At the time of my visit about 9,300. Low mark, at the bottom of the depression, employees numbered about 7,000.

These works form a complete industrial city. Number of buildings have expanded to 190. In them are 150 acres of floor space. Within the plant are approximately 9 miles of roadway and 33 miles of track on which 22 electric locomotives and 800 freight cars operate. A fleet of more than 180 automobiles and trucks, together with 1,200 trailers, enable persons and things to go places. Under the street is an elaborate system of pipes and conduits serving community needs for heat, light, water and power. The pumping system has a daily capacity of 25,000,000 gallons, exclusive of the drinking water system, and radiator and pipe coils are sufficient to heat more than 2,700 homes of average size. An automatic telephone system utilizes 3,500 instruments. The works has its own police, fire department and hospital. Twelve men sleep in the firehouse nightly. In the hospital are five doctors. The services of the medical staff and facilities of the hospital are free to employees. Every prospective employee must undergo a rigid examination, including the Wassermann test. In 1929 the 14 restaurants operated by the Company, where food was sold at practically cost, served more than 2,000,000 meals.

In the outer office of B. L. Delack, the Works Manager, there was no waste motion. The young lady who presides over the typewriter pushed a panel in the wall, spoke through it and presently I found myself in the large inner office — severely plain and streaming with sunlight. After courteously and patiently answering all of my questions, Manager Delack turned me over to Mr. Bernhard G. Tang — "Barney" to you — the General Superintendent and he took me over the plant.

In the galleries of the turbine shop we looked down upon 35 turbines for Government destroyers, which were being brought into being. From where we stood to the opposite end of the shop the distance was 800 feet. Far up under the vast ceiling, in a little gondola, what looked like a tiny monkey in blue denim and with a bald head made mysterious motions. His duty was to guide the giant Morgan crane, weighing 40 tons and costing $60,000, which can pick up 100 tons as neatly as you can lift a match from the carpet.

On the ground floor we inspected the turbine castings, lying about like gray monsters from some prehistoric era, and witnessed the miracle of arc welding. Each casting is subjected to the piercing scrutiny of the X-ray, which registers every flaw on a photographic plate. Then the welder drills to the flaw with the electric arc and plugs it with fresh metal, in the same manner that a dentist treats a decayed tooth. Putting on my head a contraption which resembled a diver's helmet, I watched the fiery ray burn its way into the sullen metal. The heart of the flame was a dazzling white, while about it flickered a dusky, reddish cloud. When we had approached, the welder had stopped his work and as we turned away he began again. "Don't look," cautioned my guide. But like Lot's wife I *had* to look, though not for long. For an hour afterwards my eyes felt as they do when you stare into the noonday sun. It does not pay to get brash with a flame operating a temperature of nearly 3,000 degrees Fahrenheit.

Six of us from the works lunched at the Mohawk Club in the heart of Old Schenectady, near where the stockade of the first settlers once stood. In the same block was the Historical Society and a four-square old mansion across the street that might easily have been transported from Salem, Mass., so strongly did it resemble the castles of the sea captains of a century ago. I rather expected to hear much conversation about watts and "amps" and "kw's," but whether out of courtesy to me, a layman, or whether there is an unwritten rule not to talk shop at meals, the conversation ranged from golf to Wall Street and, of course, the great depression. It was no news to me to hear that those in closest touch with General Electric affairs had not "got out" at or near the top of the bull market. Everyone, of course, owned stock in the Company and no one had any doubts as to its future.

But how nice it would have been if one had sold out at, say 300 or 400 and bought the stock back under 10, as one might have done in 1932. Ten for the present stock is equivalent to 40 for the old stock which was split 4 for 1 in January, 1930. I was reminded of a little jingle that appeared in *Cosmopolitan*, which ran:

> "Kathleen Mavourneen, if I had been clever,
> The wealth of the Indies had surely been mine;
> It may be four years, but it seems like forever,
> Since General Electric was 399."

That the general public, too, has not lost faith in our greatest electric company is evidenced by the fact that on December 16, 1929 the number of stockholders totaled 60,374, a high record to that date, while on December 16, 1933 stockholders numbered 181,310, an increase of more than 200% during this period. Truly an astonishing record, considering the times. It took nine years to build the stockholders' list from 20,000 to the 60,000 total of 1929 and in the three desperate depression years which followed, 120,000 additional persons became General Electric shareholders. In the words of Ol' Man Ribber it "must mean something."

At a nearby table were a group of scientists including Dr. Irving Langmuir, winner of the last Nobel Prize and inventor of the gas-filled or Mazda "C" lamp which now supplies more than half the world's electric light. We were not near enough to hear what our neighbors were talking about, but general opinion was that their conversation was of a pretty hefty nature.

The high spots of my afternoon tour were the X-ray room, where all metal work is tested for flaws, the wire drawing plant, the refrigerator plant and finally the "House of Magic." The X-ray room is large enough to admit the biggest casting. Its walls are lined with one-half inch lead sheets. The operator shoots the ray from outside and looks into the room through a lead glass window. On the negatives the unflawed metal shows up white, while black dots or splotches give the location of flaws.

The turbine and wire-drawing plants were the busiest spots in the Schenectady works at the time of my visit. The former was a place of vast spaces and comparative silence, while the latter was filled with whirling machines whose raucous voices almost numbed the listener. In the wire plant most of the work is done by machinery, so deft and accurate that it makes human hands seem slow and clumsy. Some drew the heavy "bull" wire into varying diameters, just as one pulls taffy. Some machines shellacked wire; others wrapped it in paper, coated it with tar and oakum, or enameled it in various colors. On a whirling flat disk a dozen bobbins leaped in a sort of May-pole dance. The result was a glistening, hollow, plaited, wire cable, as flexible as a piece of rope and as glisteningly beautiful as a maiden's tresses. The raw, or "bull" wire, comes into the wire plants on huge spools; diameter one-half inch. The wire plant draws this to any desired size; smallest, two-fifths the diameter of the finest hair. A bit of it is difficult to see unless one holds it up tc the light.

Refrigerator manufacturing is a seasonal business and that plant was tapering off, as is customary at that time of the year. By January, 1934, this department will again be at full blast and giving employment to several thousand additional workmen.

The "House of Magic," which is, in reality, two buildings containing approximately 100 rooms, deserves its name. Properly to describe its achievements would require volumes — not pages — and most of it would be intelligible only to those with scientific training. In this Research Laboratory, which is the official title, the technique of working brittle tungsten was developed; this made possible the tungsten incandescent lamp. Dr. Langmuir's work in electrons gave us the radio power tube, the heart of the broadcasting station. He also invented atomic-hydrogen welding, a process giving the hottest and most intensely reducing flame yet produced, and the Thyraton, a grid-controlled arc device finding important uses as relay, current regulator and converter from direct to alternating current.

Dr. W. D. Coolidge, Director of the Research Laboratory, invented the Coolidge X-ray tube which has displaced many former types, and the high-power cathode-ray tube, a new and powerful instrument for the physicist and perhaps for the surgeon. Dr. E. F. W. Alexanderson has been a leader in the development of the radio and television. C. A. Hoxie and H. B. Marvin were largely responsible for the development of the Photophone Talking Movie, while C. W. Rice and E. W. Kellogg developed the dynamic-type loudspeaker, which is now extensively used for high quality reproduction as well as for the talking-movie sound reproduction. This list of scientists is far from complete, but space forbids. To enumerate in the briefest way the total of miracles accomplished and in process would require many pages.

A Wisconsin '29 graduate took me through the "House of Magic." In one room studies were in progress in reference to the heat effects of short waves, used in producing artificial fevers. In another, experiments were showing the effects of X-rays on plant life. At one place my guide exhibited an electric fan which operates as noiselessly as a moth's wings, and at another place the "electric eye" which never fails to discriminate between black and white. Here also is a new kind of magnet, as light as a feather but ten times more powerful than an ordinary magnet of the same size. Perhaps through this, entire fields may be revolutionized.

Another room glowed with an unearthly radiance. Here dozens of the new sodium-vapor lamps are being tested. This lamp, which emits a beautiful, yellow light, is three times more powerful than

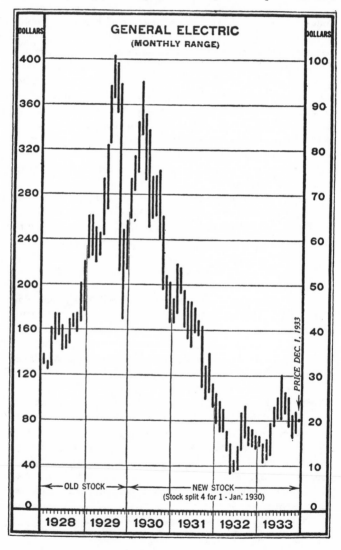

an ordinary tungsten lamp of the same size. The sodium-vapor lamp is not yet commercially practical, but its potentialities are tremendous.

In the research laboratory are also conducted elaborate studies in the realms of pure science, i.e., abstract science without thought of commercial objectives; for to limit the field of research would be to limit the field of possible achievement.

I have made only occasional reference to the care and solicitude the Company shows towards its employees. Under that head come devices and regulations for protection against injury, hospitals, restaurants, workmen's accident compensation, the mutual benefit association, the savings and investment plan, supplementary compensation, group life insurance, pensions, housing and home building, athletics, recreation, educational courses, student engineering, electrical courses, apprentice courses, libraries and a relief and loan plan. The Company's attitude is not that of paternalism but of coöperation. Hence, labor troubles are exceedingly rare.

My little visit to the Schenectady works was not to study the details of electrical manufacture. That would have taken weeks. My chief purpose was to observe General Electric's biggest unit in actual operation and therefrom to estimate the character of the entire organization. I went away with the conviction that I had seen a great plant running "under wraps," to use a racing term, owing to unfavorable economic conditions. None of the qualities and abilities which built General Electric to its present mighty stature are lacking today. It has the money, the management, the creative ability, the organization, the plant and the skilled labor necessary to perpetuate its growth. Here is no case of a worn-out dynasty. We are living in an electrical age, which General Electric has been a most important factor — perhaps *the* most important factor — in creating. In the writer's humble opinion the electrical age has hardly more than begun. When the economic tide turns, if indeed, it has not already turned, General Electric is in a position to ride on its crest.

To Readers: Do you like this article? Do you wish us to publish others of the same kind?

EDITOR.

Annuities—The Foundation of Financial Independence

This department will be conducted by Mr. David A. Lunden-Moore.

THE principle of investing money is not as simple as it appears; particularly for the average man or woman. Very often a man will make great sacrifices to save a substantial sum that will make his declining years secure, only to lose all through ill-advised investments.

The most skillful investors are frequently baffled by the violent fluctuations of security markets and sudden changes in the fortunes of business enterprises. Billions of dollars have been lost by men and women in useless and unsound investments and in other financial undertakings during the last few years.

But the foundation of a fortune can always be had in the annuity — a contract which guarantees a fixed income for life.

That our people are beginning to appreciate the true worth of annuities is shown by their phenomenal growth in the past few years. In 1927, $60,000,000. In 1929, $99,000,000. In 1932, almost $200,000,000.

One has but to meet with the man or woman who derives an income from an annuity in order to appreciate the blessings of such an investment. Throughout our country there are thousands upon thousands of such people who, for the rest of their lives, will receive income checks month after month. You can find them in the big cities, in small country places, on luxury liners going around the world.

These people enjoy life in peace and contentment. It is a recognized fact that annuitants, as a group, enjoy a longer span of life than the average person. The annuitant is as free as the air, dependent on no one, but equipped to enjoy leisure according to his or her fancy.

What the annuity can do for you, and its place in your investment program, is illustrated in a chart which we shall be glad to send you on request.

Typical Letters Received by a Prominent Life Insurance Company

HER ONLY INCOME SINCE THE DEPRESSION

What a pleasure it is for me to tell you how much I appreciate my Annuity. It has been my only income since the depression. I think it's the only safe investment for a woman alone to have. Such is my case. Without my Annuity my home would have to go, along with everything else. I talk Annuities to everyone that I think can or should have one.   L. V. T., Lenox, Mass.

JUDGMENT OF FRIENDS JUSTIFIED

My experience with the Insurance Company has most certainly justified the judgment of other people in guiding the purchase of my Annuity at a time when I did not know what was best for my own interest. After the lapse of years, I can now state that a life insurance Annuity in a good company is one of the best of investments. I have taken not only satisfaction but real comfort in the regularity and certainty of payments. No improvement can be made as far as I am concerned.   E. C. D., Valley Stream, N. Y.

TYPICAL QUESTION AND ANSWER

Question: About five years ago I invested $108,000 in what I thought were sound securities. I had a comfortable income and was about ready to retire from business. Suddenly conditions began to change. Upon the advice of a friend I switched from one security to another. Now I am puzzled. My income today is less than $700 a year. I can still salvage about $55,000 in cash. I am advised to buy an Annuity. I have been told that at my age, 62, I can get about $400 a month. Is this income guaranteed for life? Will the income fluctuate? Do I have to pay taxes on my income?

Answer: By investing $55,000 at age 62 your income will be over $5,000 a year. You can receive your checks annually, semi-annually, quarterly or monthly. You will receive somewhat more on an annual basis than semi-annually or quarterly. This sum is absolutely guaranteed without the slightest fluctuation and is payable for life. Your income is entirely free from taxation for a period of about $10\frac{1}{2}$ years. Annuities are the safest investment in the world and we have no hesitation in recommending them.

HAS INCREASED INCOME THREE TIMES

I had my money invested in government bonds and different banks. Two years ago I purchased an Annuity and the following year I bought another one. By making the exchange I have increased my income three times. Also I consider it the best investment for a person of my age.   W. M. C., St. Johnsbury, Vt.

HAS ADVISED FRIENDS TO BUY ANNUITIES

In 1925, at the age of sixty-one, I bought an Annuity and since then have received an income amounting to about 9.6% annually. The payments arrive as surely and regularly as the first of each month. I shudder to think of what might have happened if I had bought stocks. I have often advised friends to consider this kind of investment.

N. O., Minneapolis, Minn.

High Spots
In a Wall Street Career

This condensed series is from Mr. Wyckoff's autobiography "Wall Street Ventures and Adventures Through 40 Years." It will be continued through several more issues.

1904　Up from the Lows — *Continued*

AS a result of my study of the market and the various stocks, I issued a brief market letter. In this, it will be noted, the buying point in United States Steel common was put down as around $10 per share, and I mentioned it because, whether they admitted it or not, many held it at 40 or 50. The letter follows:

June, 1904.

I've been a bear for two years, but I'm a bear no longer.

The return of investment capital to Wall Street, the splendid crop outlook, and the growth of confidence in the election of a "safe" President, are unquestionably forerunners of a bull market. And it will be here before you realize it, so don't procrastinate.

Here are the best things to buy:

READING, because it's earning 8½% on the common and will probably pay a dividend in the fall. Three-quarters of this stock is "out of the market," and the balance is being steadily accumulated. Besides, it's only a few points from the lowest in three years.

UNION PACIFIC COMMON, earning four times its dividend, to say nothing of its equity in Southern Pacific. It is far cheaper than St. Paul, N. Y. Central or Pennsylvania, and in good times will pay an increased dividend. What's more, it's a market leader, and something you can hand down to the children, so far as income is concerned.

ATCHISON, earning 10% and paying 4%. The cheapest of the active standard stocks. No reason why it should be eight points below Baltimore & Ohio and sixteen points below Union Pacific.

FRISCO 2nd, the lowest 4% dividend payer on the railroad list. Nets nearly 9% on the investment, sells at 46, earning over thrice the dividend, and still showing increases. Close to lowest in some years.

STEEL 5s, should go to 85 on the least revival in the trade. By the way, *better average up on Steel Common around 10.*

MISSOURI, KANSAS & TEXAS PREFERRED, earning over 8%. The big cotton crop should bring a dividend on this stock. The common, too, is dirt cheap (16½). Lowest in recent years 14⅝.

The big men are accumulating stocks. Better follow suit. You can't buy at the lowest eighth — neither can they. *GET BULLISH.*

I had turned from bear to bull just in time. No sooner had I issued this market letter than the market began to climb. It was as though I had got on the last car of the last train just before it pulled out of the station.

The market advanced for two years. Within this period Reading, which had begun dividend payments on a 4 per cent basis, sold at 164. Union Pacific increased its dividend rate to $10 per share, and in a tremendous 60-point advance, within a very short time, surged up to 195¼. Both Atchison and St. Louis & San Francisco 2nd Pfd. nearly doubled in price. Missouri, Kansas & Texas common rose during that period to 40⅝ and U. S. Steel common to 50½.

* * *

The firm of Mallett & Wyckoff made money. Within a year it had the reputation of being an active and growing house. It was more than ordinarily successful in guiding its clients, but I was not satisfied as to this.

Advising clients of a stock brokerage house is one of the most difficult tasks anyone can undertake. Almost anyone with some years of experience in Wall Street can be correct in his judgment from time to time; but the problem is to be correct *most* of the time.

Having learned to get business by mail, I was ambitious to make a great success of the advisory part of the work. If I should gain the reputation of having better judgment than the average broker, I could then secure and hold a large and growing clientele.

I was thirty years old now; had accumulated some capital, but I had overworked for many years. I decided to lessen my responsibilities and find more time for my study of the stock market. So along in 1904, I dissolved partnership with Mallett and hooked up with the firm of Ashwell & Company, members of the New York Stock Exchange. I brought my clientele over with me and began to devote five or six hours a day to looking after it.

My friends would say: "What a lot of changes you make in business!" My answer would be: "A rolling stone is worth two in the bush."

Ashwell was a good friend of James R. Keene, whose office was in the same building. Many a good bit of information came out of Ashwell's daily calls upon the eminent speculator.

My new business brought me in about $18,000 a year, which was all right so far as making a living was concerned. But my main concern still was to get at the inside of the Wall Street works. Nothing was too much trouble if it would help me accomplish this.

1905   Studying the Big Fellows

The firm of Wasserman Bros. was prominent in what I suspected to be the manipulation of Reading. In order to find out what was going on in that office, I got my friend Mallett to open a speculative account there.

Wasserman Bros. seemed to have better information on Reading than on anything else, and this information seemed to be better than that possessed by any other house. I knew the firm had a number of big clients, but who these were I did not know. I decided to find out.

After Mallett had become acquainted, I asked him to tell Edward Wasserman that he knew a man with quite a clientele who wished to talk over the possibility of connecting himself with the firm. Wasserman said that he would like to see me; and I had a talk with him. With the result that I moved my hat from Ashwell's over to Wasserman Bros. I had accepted a fixed salary of $1,000 a month. This was a sacrifice of $6,000 a year, but I felt it would be worth that.

Soon, I began to nose around to see what I could learn. The

firm had the reputation of being a Morgan house because they were more active in Reading than in any other stock. Frequently the news ticker would contain items to the effect that Wasserman Bros. had bought 25,000 or 50,000 Reading. They always seemed to be on the buying side of that stock. Further acquaintance disclosed the fact that Edward Wasserman was more or less obsessed with the bullish possibilities of Reading. It did not take me long to find out how all this had started.

The preceding year, Edward Wasserman had gone on a trip abroad. His first stop was London. There he met J. P. Morgan, who told him the Reading Company was "through spending money on the property; now the stockholders were going to be rewarded." "Eddie" immediately bought himself a big line of Reading by cable, and jumped on the next steamer going home.

Arriving in New York, he went to Dick Canfield's gambling house on 44th Street, next to Delmonico's, and told the noted gambler about it. Canfield immediately gave him an order to buy 25,000 shares of Reading, and later 25,000 more. Wasserman then went to Kessler, and Kessler gave him a big order. He loaded up his other clients, then disclosed the information to large floor traders like Jakey Field and Billy Oliver, who immediately went long of Reading.

Wasserman's methods, when he got one or more of these big orders — and usually he tried to bunch them — was to go into the Reading crowd and make his purchases in a loud and sensational manner, giving the effect that he was sent in to corral all the capital stock. Whether he actually did buy all the round lots of Reading that were credited to him I cannot state. But so long as the news tickers, news slips and newspapers gave him the publicity he was well satisfied.

Reading, under this impetus, began to climb into the 50s, 60s and 70s. There appeared to be no inside stock for sale, judging from the ease with which Reading mounted to new highs.

As the stock began to approach 100, the big floor traders that Wasserman had brought in, and the general public, began to think this was too high. Large lines of shorts were put out. Wasserman kept close tab on the demand for Reading in the stock loan crowd. Whenever he saw the short interest extended, he told clients Reading was going to have another big move, got a lot of orders, and going into the crowd, loudly executed them. The shorts would then fear they were going to lose their pants; they covered quickly. Their buying would help Eddie's game, and when they bid it up high enough, he let them have some of the stock.

Although the Street was under the impression that Wasserman was buying most of this stock for Morgan, I could never make sure that he bought one share for the house on the corner. If he did, everybody took great pains to conceal the fact. This was not Morgan's way of doing, anyway. This great financier had a private office of his own uptown, from which his stock market campaigns were conducted; and while he did frequently use Reading to punish the shorts and stiffen the market, his bidding up was not done by Wasserman.

While the latter always claimed that he never had a pool in Reading — and I believe this was true — some of his moves looked like pool manipulation. One strong reason for the Street's pool theory was Eddie's habit of bidding for round lots of stock. He would go into the Reading crowd with an order to buy 10,000 or 20,000 shares, which might have been all or partly for himself, or made up of a number of orders from clients, and after executing these orders as carefully as the market would permit, he would end up in one grand spectacular bid for 25,000 shares.

He really had no such order and the bid was solely for effect. (The rules of the Stock Exchange have since been revised so that a broker bidding for a round lot must accept all or any part of the amount bid for. But the rules at the time permitted one to bid for a round lot without having to accept less.) Making his big bid, Wasserman knew pretty well that no one would fill it.

The bullish effect on the traders in the Reading crowd and in the brokerage offices would be greatly emphasized by the news items which appeared on the slips and news tickers and, later, in the newspapers: "Wasserman pool bids for 25,000 share lots of Reading and gets none." These items led many outside buyers to go into Reading and often Wasserman and his clients realized an almost immediate profit.

Reading worked up to around 110. Hereabout Canfield took a profit of several hundred thousand dollars on 25,000 shares of his stock.

It was also about at this level that George A. Kessler and some of his friends conceived the idea of cornering Reading. They began to make large purchases of the stock. Some of these orders were given to Wasserman; he executed them in his best style, with a great blowing of trumpet, but he told me he was skeptical as to the ability of the pool to corner the stock.

Reading climbed another 10 or 20 points, and the excitement increased. Followers of the Kessler party worked like Trojans trying to induce everyone to buy Reading. It "was going to $200, to $300 — no telling how high! They were going to corner it!" They seemed to have stolen Eddie Wasserman's thunder and multiplied it several times.

When the stock had reached 135, Wasserman asked me to call up Canfield at his gambling house in Saratoga, to tell him where Reading was, and ask him if he wanted to do anything. Canfield gave me an order to sell his remaining 25,000 shares. The order was executed in the neighborhood of 136 and his profit on the two lots was approximately $2,000,000.

Kessler and his crowd went on bulling until Reading hit 164. Then suddenly it looked as though Morgan, the First National Bank, H. C. Frick and all the other big boys had simply opened the floodgates to let those ambitious chaps have all the Reading they wanted.

Reading took a quick flop of fifty points. The pool went home badly spanked and thoroughly discouraged. The real insiders undoubtedly bought back at the low levels what they had sold, for a heavy buying movement around 112 now rallied the stock.

With Reading under 120, Eddie got very bullish again. He bought a lot of the stock himself and started in to collect orders from his big clients and such pool members as had not been cleaned out in the break. But one day a telephone message came from a secretary at "the corner" to the effect that "Mr. Morgan would like to see Mr. Wasserman."

First he tiptoed around the office and informed everyone, in a mysterious whisper: "Mr. Morgan wants to see me." Then he went to his wardrobe and took down the high silk hat which he kept for such occasions. And after he was all shined, brushed and polished, he started over to Headquarters.

He was back in fifteen minutes, greatly subdued. In the same

Continued on page VI

Excerpts from "The Law of Financial Success"

MONEY means freedom, independence, liberty. It means the opportunity to carry out great plans and to fulfill great ideals. It means the filling in of those mental pictures that we have sketched out in our minds. It means the chance of materializing those airy "Castles in Spain" that we have dwelt upon in moments of hopeful ecstasy. Money is the wizard, able and willing to work wonders. It is indeed, the genie who can and will do its master's bidding.

I hold that in the present stage of evolution of man, money is to mankind what air, water, sunshine and mother-earth are to the plant — it is *Nourishment*. And, as in the plant, the desire for nourishment is a natural and worthy instinct, so is the desire for this financial nourishment in man a perfectly natural and worthy instinct — it is the working of the same natural law. And, mark you this, that as the desire of the plant is a natural indication of the existence of the nourishment-need, so is this desire in the breast of man a certain indication of the possibility of its satisfaction and attainment, if natural laws are but followed. Nature is no mocker — it causes no desire to spring up in a living thing, unless it also endows that living thing with the faculties and powers to attain that which it craves. A realization of this great natural law will do many of my readers much good just now.

But note this, also, nature does not encourage the hoarding up of anything for the mere sake of acquisition. It punishes this error severely. The LAW OF USE underlies all of nature's instinctive cravings. It desires that the living thing shall draw to itself the nourishment and material it needs, in order to *use* it. And this desire for money on the part of man is governed by this same law — the Law of Use. Nature wishes you to desire money — to attract it to you — to possess and acquire it — and lastly, and most important of all, *to use it*. By using money, and keeping it working and in action, you will fall in line with the workings of this great Law of Use. By falling in with this Law, you work in harmony with the great natural forces and purposes.

Flashes

THEY walk with speed who walk alone.

A rolling stock is worth two in the bush.

A plunger makes big money at times, but seldom keeps it.

The best equipped man in the Street is the fellow who wears earmuffs.

Philosophy of Edward H. Harriman

Grasp an idea and work it out to a successful conclusion; that's about all there is in life for any of us.

To achieve what the world calls success a man must attend strictly to business and keep a little in advance of the times.

The man who reaches the top is the one who is not content with doing just what is required of him. He does more.

Every man should make up his mind that if he expects to succeed, he must give an honest return for the other man's dollar.

Continued from page 42

mysterious whispers he told us all that we were to keep very quiet about Reading from now on. Mr. Morgan did not want any more excitement in the stock. His reason was clear. During Wasserman's bull campaign from the 40s to the 160s he had let it ride. But now, having dumped about all the Reading in the World on the Kessler pool, he naturally wanted to buy it back below 120. Without any bull leader the stock went through that well-known period of rest and quiet near the bottom of its down swing.

Other installments will follow

Some Comments on the Proposed Stock Exchange Legislation

By RICHARD D. WYCKOFF

PRESIDENT ROOSEVELT is right in stating that "unnecessary, unwise and destructive speculation should be eliminated." Unnecessary speculation is continually practiced by those who know little or nothing about it; who cannot afford to speculate, and whose operations are not justified from any standpoint. This also properly describes unwise speculation. And there is a necessity for eliminating destructive speculation for it is this element which has contributed so heavily to the present legislative crisis.

Few people will agree with the President that "it should be our national policy to restrict as far as possible the use of the Exchanges for purely speculative operations." Why should it? Were it not for purely speculative operations the development of the United States as a manufacturing, industrial and agricultural nation could never have reached its highest levels. Speculation is characteristic of practically every line of business in America; it is not possible to get away from this fact. Our great industrials could never have been financed on an investment basis alone. Furthermore, speculation in stocks intelligently conducted is a very important industry in this country, and should be fostered.

It is difficult to understand how the President or Congress can take such a stand against speculation in face of the fact that Uncle Sam has been and is today the world's largest speculator. Not long ago he was using the public funds in artificially supporting the market for wheat and cotton;

his losses ran into hundreds of millions of dollars. The Government is right now involved in the most gigantic speculations the world has ever seen. It has captured gold; manipulated the price to a fifty per cent higher level by continually raising the bid. It has established a fund of two billion dollars out of the paper profits in the gold operations and has undertaken to stabilize the price of American exchange in foreign markets. Who knows? We might lose the two billions just as we lost vast sums in the cotton and grain markets.

And now the President and Congress are dictating to the people: You shall not do in a small way what we are doing on a gigantic scale with your money. It is all right for us but not for you. Yet the identical principle is involved.

It would be well for those in authority to consult their dictionaries as to the meaning of the word, "speculation." Mine says: "A risky investment for large profit." If anyone entertains the idea that the Stock Exchange is primarily a place where investors may buy and be protected, and where speculation has no place, they are sadly misinformed. Pure investment involves the placing of money solely for safety of principal and surety of income. When to these objectives even a small percentage of desire for profit is added, a speculative motive exists, and that is what distinguishes real investment from speculation; it is not the payment for stocks in full. Speculative operations on the Stock Exchange are a form of merchandising, the purpose of which is to derive a profit from price changes; to buy at a lower price than one sells. I defy Washington to prove that the majority of our people who deal in stocks are not seeking profit. And if that be the case, the Government in endeavoring to dictate: "Thou shalt not," is putting itself much in the same position as it did with the Eighteenth Amendment.

There is no question as to the need for protection from highly organized and powerful insiders possessing advance information and from pools and cliques who mark and stack the cards against a weak, mostly uninformed and certainly unorganized mass of outsiders. Perhaps the proposed Bill will add some measure of such protection.

The demand for higher margins will not stop people from speculating, or "investing," as many of them call it. It will merely reduce the number of shares in which they trade.

Prohibition of manipulation by means of raising or depressing prices, creating false markets, should result in a more natural market; but under such a ruling prices will be more unstable especially in periods of stress. As shown in the panic of 1929, stabilization is at times the only thing that stands between comparative safety and complete demoralization.

Spreading of rumors, paying for printed propaganda and the many evils coming under this head should be under better control.

Abolishing of corners is a wise move but not for the reasons our legislators have in mind. It will open the way to more general trading on the short as well as the long side of the market. This will lend an element of stabilization that will be supplied by the public, most of whom now hesitate to sell short for fear of corners. If Congress but knew it, encouraging short selling would aid in preventing such violent upward movements as we had in 1929. That was because all the passengers were on one side and the boat turned over.

The right to use and trade against options is evidently based on a distorted idea of what part these play in legitimate Wall Street operations. No good purpose will be served by restricting the sale or purchase of options, or the trading against them, provided they are issued by those who are limited to certain quantities of shares or commodities to a point where they are well able to handle them.

Control of short sales and stop orders cannot be intelligently discussed until (if, as and when) the Bill becomes a law, and it is known what the Commission's requirements will be; but it would be extremely unfortunate if appointees to that Commission were unfamiliar with Stock Exchange machinery relating to these two practices and were allowed to throw their theoretical and probably mistaken requirements into that machinery. To remove an artificial means of stabilization by cutting out manipulation is one thing; to choke off natural and legitimate processes of steadying the stock market would be another — and a gross error. Such a provision would defeat its own purpose.

Opening brokers' records to inspection by the Commission would be on a par with a demand, say, that attorneys disclose all the intimate details of their clients' affairs. Such has always been the relationship between broker and client. Giving a Government Commission power to snoop through brokers' books would undoubtedly lead to the formation of cliques operated through or informed by members of the Commission for their own personal benefit on the basis of inside information thus obtained. Should this provision be included in the law, we may well expect a new investigating committee to be formed for the purpose of examining into the stock market operations traceable to members of the proposed Commission.

There are some constructive features in the Bill. No one will deny the necessity for certain reforms, especially those which the Stock Exchange has heretofore been unable to control because of operations conducted outside of the Exchange and mostly by those not connected with it. Such a regulation as is proposed, if it becomes a law, will quite naturally reduce the volume of trading because much of the activity heretofore has had its base in pool operations; but there have been and will again be times when the public will become so powerful a factor in the market as to minimize the dealings of large operators. Possibly the margin restrictions will have the effect of reducing on such occasions what might develop into unbridled and, as the President has put it, "unnecessary, unwise and destructive speculation."

Take a Tip from the Flea

Great Fleas have Little Fleas
  Upon their backs to bite 'em:
And Little Fleas have Lesser Fleas,
  And so, *ad infinitum.*

THE writer of the foregoing undoubtedly was not thinking of the Stock Market at the time he penned his lines.
And yet, we have in the sentiment which they express, at
least the embryonic idea which perhaps has more to do with
the relative success or failure of the small trader, than almost
any other condition. But what, you may well ask, have fleas
to do with the Stock Market, or the market with fleas?

In order to investigate this somewhat delicate point, let
us consider for a few moments the ways of the Flea, and how
he goes about the problem of gaining a livelihood. Due
to a long residence in certain foreign countries where bath-
tubs are not too numerous, I have on many occasions come
into intimate and, sad to say, even personal contact with
these interesting if pestiferous insects. I can therefore claim a
certain degree of expert knowledge on this subject.

In the first place (all market traders should note this carefully), the Flea is a live wire, and is always on the job looking
for opportunities which spell profit for him. And in the pur-
suit of such profit, and the general conduct of his business,
whenever he moves, he moves *quickly*, and *with decision.*
Whether the cause of his moves be the desire for food in the
form of warm, red blood (more profit), or whether it be to
get out of the way of the angry "swat" of his victim (danger),
doesn't make a particle of difference to Mr. John H. Flea.
Whenever he moves, he jumps so quickly, and so far, that
you are not likely to see him again until he draws your attention to his presence by a further subtraction of your life's
blood, for which he leaves you in return, a pretty little round
irritated red spot on your delicate skin.

This stays with you for days and days, and is a constant reminder of how Mr. Flea put it over on you.

The first thing therefore, which traders should learn from the Flea, is that when it is time to make a move (a) into the market for profit, or (b) out to protect yourself from danger, let that move be like the Flea's — quick, clean and decisive. A Flea never vacillates; every move has a purpose behind it. And as a result of his moves, and his quickness in making them, the flea gains a very satisfactory living for a small outlay of effort, and at minimum risk to himself. If you don't believe his risk is small, just try to catch a flea!

But in addition to the way he makes his moves, the Flea has an even more valuable lesson for the small trader. The Flea never works hard for his living; that is, figuratively speaking, he never bothers to plant the ground, and reap the harvest, or go through a lot of silly motions. Oh, no! Mr. Flea is much too wise. He leaves all that for foolish men to do; and when men have planted the ground, and reaped the harvest, and manufactured the product into food, and then eaten the food and turned it into good, satisfactory blood — this is Mr. Flea's opportunity. If there is one thing the Flea loves more than another, it is good, rich, thick, red and warm human blood! In other words, the Flea believes in letting the other fellow do the hard work, and he just cashes in on the result!

Now the Flea is very selective in his tastes, just as traders should be in stocks. For instance, there are some fleas that go in for cats and dogs, and never rise above this stage. There are some traders in this class also. But the really high class flea — what we might describe as the "human" flea, because he rides with human beings in preference to cats and dogs — this is the flea "de luxe," the one which we as traders should strive to emulate.

The Human Flea, goes in for quality blood, such as for instance, can be found flowing in the veins of Big, Strong, Stout, Market Operators. Whenever he is lucky enough to see one of these, Mr. Flea wastes no time whatever, but promptly proceeds to fasten himself on the most inaccessible portion of the Big Operator's back, where he can neither be reached nor shaken off. In other words, whenever and wherever the Big Operator moves, the Flea moves right along with him. The Big Operator does all the work and assumes all the responsibility, while the Flea feasts in solid comfort! And while the Big Operator at times finds a collection of such fleas on his back very annoying, and resorts to "shake-outs," and other similar tricks to rid himself of them, if the Flea knows the tricks of the Big Operator as he should, there is relatively small danger of being shaken off.

But how does the Flea know who is a Big Operator, and who isn't? The answer is that the Flea doesn't care a continental whether or not he has a speaking acquaintance with the Big Operator, or whether he even knows his name. He doesn't need to know him personally. But he can tell by certain well known signals (resulting from manipulation) that Big Operator is *in the market*, and when he sees these signals, he goes after him, and attaches himself to Big Operator, rides with him right through the campaign, and has the best of meals and service provided free of charge!

Now, reader, rough or gentle, this is where you can take a tip from the Flea. You know that there are Big Operators in the Market. And if you learn how to recognize the trail they invariably must leave behind them in carrying out their stunts, you can make of yourself, as far as your market operations are concerned, a Human Flea. You can ride along with the Big Operator, following his moves, getting in on the profits which are made possible by his campaign, and getting out when he gets out.

How is it possible to do this? There is only one way: by being able to interpret what the ticker tape reveals. On this thin little ribbon, for five hours each day, is registered the combined opinion of all, big and little, whether they be investors, speculators or merely gamblers, as to the probable effect on any stock, of all the business, political and financial, or any other forces which are liable to change stock prices in any way. Here then, you have the world's most expert opinion passing before you hourly and daily, as to the probable movement of any particular stock, or of the market as a whole. But what good is such an opinion if you cannot interpret it accurately?

If you are one of those poor unfortunates known to your friends as a "wise guy," you will at this point in our discussion throw this magazine in the waste basket, with some remark such as "boloney!" or its equivalent in stronger language, with the added observation that it is impossible to get anything but history of past performance from the tape; that it indicates nothing as to the future. But if, on the other hand, you realize that everybody does not lose in the market, and that those who make a good thing out of it, do so not because of luck, but rather *because they know the rules of the game.*

You have probably visited often the Customers' Room of your Broker. If you have studied the heterogeneous and gossipy crowd around you, you will have noted that there are usually two or three men who have little to say to their neighbors, who never ask anyone's opinion as to what the market is likely to do, who make a trade occasionally, and who usually make money. These men know the rules. They read the tape and interpret what the figures show them; and by knowing, they are able to recognize what the Big Operators are trying to do. By following along with the Big Operators in this way, they are able to make a satisfactory income, with very little effort on their part.

So take a lesson from the Flea, who at one time did not know how to take a bite out of anything.

While not in any sense an exact science, the stock market is, in the last analysis, a study in the forces which raise and lower prices, all of which are expressed in the Law of Supply and Demand, the only real fundamental factor.

It's Not the *Kind* of a Chart

But Your Ability to Interpret That Counts

ENDLESS discussion goes on as to which kind of a chart is best. The answer in everyone's case is this: The chart to use is the one that helps you to make the most money in the market; and if you have a combination of charts that get a better result than a single one or kind, then it is best to follow the one that pays you the most for your efforts.

Charts are useless to those who cannot read or interpret them. But they have great value to traders who understand them, because they constantly reflect the relation of Supply and Demand.

Properly constructed charts are just as valuable to the trader and the student of the market, as the records of the instruments in a power plant are valuable to the operator of such a plant. They show what is going on now and what is likely to happen in the future — near or distant.

Charts reflect the development of forces that are likely to act as soon as they are strong enough to overcome the resistance that opposes them. They present in graphic form accumulated evidence as to whether or not this resistance will be overcome.

In a certain sense, reading charts is like reading music, in which you endeavor to interpret correctly the composer's ideas and the expression of his art. Just so a chart of the averages, or of a single stock, reflects the ideas, hopes, ambitions and purposes of the mass mind operating in the market, or of a manipulator handling a single stock.

The study of charts is not as some people claim, the mere identification of certain labelled patterns made by the action of stocks. That sort of thing borders on the mechanical and does little to aid in the development of one's judgment. But when a student undertakes to read from his charts the purposes and the objective of those who are responsible for a stock's action in the market, he is beginning to see, in a true light, the meaning of scientific stock speculation.

Misleading Wall Street Expressions

That You Can't Go Broke Taking a Profit

TRUE. But you can lose a lot of big profits by taking small ones.

One big secret about money-making in stocks is to possess the judgment and the patience to let your profits run. The other half of the twin argument is, of course, you must cut your losses short.

Actually, it is silly to say you can't go broke taking a profit. What's more, that very expression often induces traders to get out before they should.

In a brokerage house recently, I heard a woman trader give an order to buy 100 shares at the market and as soon as she got her report she instructed the broker to "sell at a 2 point profit, G. T. C." She did not use a stop order.

This woman was a typical gambler. In attempting to make a small profit, she opened the way for a 10 or 20 point loss — 5 to 10 times the amount of her prospective profit. She might pile up a lot of these small profits (less commissions and taxes) while the market is strong, but the time will come when the stocks that do not move two points in her favor will doubtless show an aggregate loss larger than the total of her small profits. Thus the money she makes is only being loaned to her.

In some cases she might make twenty to fifty points profit by hanging on.

The Tape Is the Best Guide

DEAR SKEPTIC: You express doubt as to the value of any technical factors in predicting market movements under current conditions involving highly unstable currency, governmental influences, inflationary policies, etc. But you are completely overlooking the essential influences which bring about price movements of securities.

The Law of Supply and Demand *never fails* and it is the only safe guide under these extraordinary conditions. No one can judge the probable trend of the market from the study of fundamental statistics, economic changes or political developments, with any continued success.

Practically all knowledge which becomes public property, all discussions of current developments as they appear in the public press, and all so-called fundamental statistics are usually discounted days, weeks and months in advance. These influences, together with many important developments which never become public, are combined into a single resultant force which expresses itself in the temporary balance between supply and demand. Facts relating to this resultant force are presented from hour to hour and day to day on the ticker tape. Demand for and supply of the various securities increases and decreases. Adjustments and readjustments are disclosed in the form of price movements, volume changes and activity ratios. All these are available to anyone who will take the trouble to observe them and make the analysis that leads to their logical and proper interpretation.

"Losses have been just as severe, perhaps more severe, in the securities that people studied carefully and devoted a great deal of attention to, as they have in those they took on the hit-and-miss principle." — *Wiggin.*

Taking Advice on the Stock Market

STOCK market participants for the most part play the game by running around among each other, passing along tips, lies, rumors, hunches, opinions and what not, infecting each other with the germs of their ultimate losses. This is quite the opposite of what they do in their own lines of business.

Depending on the advice of others is a widespread public weakness. Imagine the publishers of the *Saturday Evening Post* begging or buying from other publishers opinions, advice, inside information, etc., on how to publish a magazine; or a woolen manufacturer taking advice from a competitor as to what kind of raw material would be best, and which kind of finished goods will probably have the best market next week or next month! This advisory phase of Wall Street practice would be an absurdity were it to be applied in other fields. Suppose someone claiming experience in regard to B.V.D.'s advertises like this:

We have the very latest information as to what the B.V.D. market is going to do in the next ten days. We have been told confidentially by one of the leading anatomists that certain new food products now being put upon the market are about to bring such changes in the human form that new designs in B.V.D.'s along certain lines will be in greatest demand. Manufacturers who take our advisory service at $100 a year in advance will gain an immediate benefit from this information. A sharp rise in B.V.D.'s is inevitable, but you must have the right shapes and sizes or you might just as well not be in the market.

P.S. If no one happens to be in the office when you call, just throw the money over the transom.

Suppose instead of taking one such advisory service a manufacturer in a certain field decided to take several, so he would "know everything that is going on." Imagine his state of mind after reading and attempting to digest all these conflicting advices, theories and forecasts. He would be in the delicate position of having to decide whether to follow the man whose chart of business conditions indicated that a mountain was in process of making, or another service that was equally positive we must expect a valley. The fact that in certain cases these charts might have adjustable spinal columns would make no impression upon him, for after all, he wants to know what to buy and what to make, so he can sell at a profit: Instead of using his own business brains he hires a lot of "experts" to come in and tinker with his business and in the end he finds the sheriff coming around to hang up the red flag.

The American people are said to be intelligent. This is true in many respects, but I cannot say it is so when it comes to their stock speculations. They believe a different brand of common sense is to be applied in Wall Street. However, many of those so often burnt in the stock market are now beginning to learn *why;* they now see that there are certain rules, regulations and requirements which they must apply in their speculations if they expect to have anything to show for their ventures. They begin to see that the man who comes into Wall Street with $50,000 to play with is apt to be without any toys after a while. On the other hand, it is increasingly apparent that the fellow who really wants to learn and can scrape up even $100 has a fair chance, if, at the outset, he recognizes the necessity for finding out what makes the wheels go round and how to make the machinery work for his benefit instead of taking his fingers off.

Just think what a pleasant and profitable game the stock market would be if the players were more or less trained to trade intelligently; to operate on the bear side as well as the bull side of the market with equal facility; to avoid being carried away by mob psychology and to refuse to fall for the designs of the manipulator! Had such a well-trained public participated in the bull market culminating in 1929, prices would never have gone so high because there would have been two camps; one opposed to the advance and the other in favor of it. The opposing bears would have cut the rise down to reasonable proportions; everybody would have had a better chance not only to make some money but to keep a fair portion of it. That is the kind of a speculative public Wall Street really needs. Their combined operations would aid rather than wreck the business of this country; they would never lose all their money in the stock market. They would not fly to the investment trusts and say: "Here are five billions of our money. Invest it for us. Take a piece out of it for yourself, but you are to stand no losses; we will take all of those."

In July last, for example, the "bull market" of 1933 was well under way. Old General Speculation was marching his troops up the hill again. Everybody was worth more than a few months ago. Equities in brokerage accounts were expanding. Released margins were being employed in taking on new commitments. Many billions in market values had been added to the New York Stock Exchange list of stocks, to say nothing of the increase in bond values.

Probably the majority of public participants in that bull market said to themselves: "I am going to see to it that they don't get me this time. When the market goes up to where I can take a good profit I am going to take it and soak the money away." Well, the record of what followed that rise was no different from its predecessors; for sure enough at the July top the public was again found with a heavy load; the inverted pyramid toppled and fell as usual.

And that sort of thing will go on and on until the public at last realizes the stock market is no place for people with some money but no knowledge of the business.

We must look upon things as they are, and not as we would wish them to be.

The Stockbroker and His Customer

Their Mutual Rights and Obligations

By Jacob Scholer *of the New York Bar*

Second Article

Is a Broker Under Any Obligation to Sell Out His Customer's Securities?

SINCE a customer's liability for his debit balance is a personal one and not limited to the securities deposited as margin, the broker is under no obligation to sell out the customer's securities when the margin has been wiped out. It is true the customer has the right at all times to require the broker to sell out the securities whether or not the margin has been exhausted, but in the absence of such orders from the customer the broker may hold the securities and rely upon the personal obligation of the customer to make good the debit balance.

It sometimes happens that after sending a sell-out notice to the customer the broker nevertheless refrains from selling the securities. Under such circumstances should the account show a further loss, is the customer still liable? The answer is, yes. The sell-out notice was sent by the broker for his benefit, not the customer's, and if the broker decides to waive it, the customer cannot be heard to complain. The fact that the customer believed that the broker would act on such notice cannot be relied on by him as being tantamount to an agreement between him and the broker to the effect that the broker should or would sell the securities; neither may the customer regard such a notice as a direction to the broker to sell.

Where, however, a broker makes an unauthorized sale, i.e., a sale made either without notice where notice was required, or a sale based upon an improper or insufficient notice, he subjects himself to a suit for damages by the customer. The measure of damages, where a wrongful sale is made, is the highest market price within a reasonable time after the customer has notice of the wrongful sale, less the amount realized on the sale. What is meant by a reasonable time is a question of fact which is often difficult to determine. A wrongful sale is regarded in law as constituting a conversion by the broker of the customer's securities.

The theory of damages to which a customer is entitled is fixed by what the customer could have purchased the stock for within a reasonable time. It does not require the customer to make the actual purchase which he might not be able to do, but merely places him in a position where he has suffered no damage by the broker's wrongful sale.

SPECIAL AGREEMENTS BETWEEN BROKER AND CUSTOMER; THEIR PURPOSE AND EFFECT

It has become general practice for brokers to enter into special written agreements with their customers. These by their terms purport to give the broker the right to sell out his customer without complying with many of the legal requirements heretofore discussed. In normal times there is usually no necessity for the broker to avail himself of the provisions of such agreements. It is only in times of panic and stress that their importance is realized. But these special agreements, unless carefully drawn and strictly adhered to, do not always afford to the broker the protection which he believes he has secured thereby.

These agreements should include authority on the part of the broker:

a. To pledge the customer's securities as margin (for an amount greater than that due from the customer), along with other securities, on the broker's general loans;

b. To close out the customer's account and sell the securities whenever the margin is deemed insufficient by the broker, without demand for margin and without notice of the closing out of the account, or of the time and place of sale;

c. To send notices which the broker may elect to send by ordinary mail or telegraph, and provide that the sending of notice in such manner shall be deemed sufficient notice. The agreement should further provide that the sending of notice in any one instance should not be deemed a waiver of the broker's right thereafter to sell without giving notice;

d. To deal with the account of any customer after his decease,

with the same rights and authority as the broker had prior
to the death of the customer, whether or not legal representatives of his estate have been appointed;

Such agreements are usually strictly construed and should be
clear and comprehensive. Thus, where a special agreement merely
reserved the right to sell "without notice" it was held that while
the broker did not have to state the time and place of sale, he was
required, nevertheless, to make a demand for additional margin,
since the requirement for such demand was not waived. The agreement should, therefore, include *both* the right to sell without notice
and the right to sell without demand for additional margin. If the
agreement is clear in this respect, it is valid and will be enforced.
The broker, however, to protect himself should procure a signed
agreement and not rely on statements contained on the back of
signature cards or monthly statements. Even though the broker
believes himself protected by his written agreement with the customer, nevertheless he often unwittingly waives provisions inserted
in the agreement for his benefit. For instance, if despite the provisions in his agreement with the customer, the broker sends out a
margin call or sell-out notice, he will be deemed to have waived the
provision in the contract that no such notice need be sent, and,
having given the customer notice, that notice must comply in
every respect with all legal requirements.

Where a customer employs a broker to purchase stocks for him
on margin, it is uniformly recognized that the broker has a right to
repledge the securities purchased, for an amount at least not ex-
ceeding the amount of his advances. The same rule, in fact, applies
to securities deposited with a broker by a customer as collateral to
secure advances for margin transactions.

While a broker may have the right to repledge the stock or
securities of his customer, it is his duty always to have available
for delivery, or within his control, stock of the *kind* and *quantity*
purchased or deposited with him by the customer, whenever full
payment for the stock is made or the indebtedness to the broker
is paid. If he repledges the customer's stock for an amount greater
than the amount owed to him by the customer (without the
customer's consent), to that extent he disables, or at least he may
disable himself from fulfilling that obligation, and there are authorities holding that such a repledge is a violation by the broker of

his duty. The broker, therefore, to be on safe ground should have a special agreement with the customer permitting the pledging of collateral for an amount greater than that due from the customer.

[*To be continued*]

Why the Dots on the Tape?

A READER asks: "There appear on the tape at different times, some items that are not preceded by dots. Sometimes there will be one dot, at other two or more. Will you please explain the significance of these markings? Some people think they are a means of tipping on these stocks. At times they appear after the price, viz., UAF 32½ . . . At other times like this: 52 . ½ . ⅝ . ¾. Occasionally the same stock runs: 52 ½ ⅝ ¾. Why this difference?"

* * *

The dots to which you refer have a very definite, practical purpose. They are used in order that transactions may not appear on the trans-lux too far behind the actual market. Thus the spacing of each transaction on the tape is increased, so that the lag between the ticker and the trans-lux screen may be reduced as much as possible.

Wherever the trans-lux is employed, there ordinarily would be a difference in time between the appearance of a transaction under the wheel of the stock ticker, and its registering on the trans-lux screen. This is because the ticker tape must travel from the wheel over a projection device which magnifies the symbols and prices and illuminates them so that they will be visible. Mechanical limitations do not allow the ticker symbols to be shown on the screen directly under the wheel. Hence there would be a lag of approximately four transactions between the ticker and the trans-lux if the dots were not used to compensate for this mechanical handicap.

The dots disappear in an active market because then the tape is traveling fast enough for the transactions to appear on the screen without an appreciable lag. When the market is very inactive and the tape halts for several seconds between sales, it is then necessary to print a string of dots so the tape will move far enough away from the stock ticker to register every transaction on the trans-lux screen as soon as it occurs.

"I have but one lamp by which my feet are guided, and that is the Lamp of Experience." — *Patrick Henry*.

Small Swings Total More Than Big Moves?

ONCE I ascertained by means of an elaborate campaign the most desirable thing to know about the stock market in the opinion of the public. It turned out to be: How to buy low and sell high. This shows what mistaken ideas the public holds about the market. The ideal operation in their minds would be to buy American Telephone and Telegraph at its low point of the depression, in 1932, say around 71, and sell it two months later at its high, 121. That would be a 50-point rise, and anyone accomplishing such a feat would never let his family or friends hear the last of it.

But there is much more to the market than this: In the months of June, July and early September, Telephone declined from around 90 to 71; then rose to 121. In making these moves, there were numerous gyrations of 5 points and over, which totalled 172 points; so that the person realizing only 50 points secured less than a third of the movements that took place during the period named.

You might say: That is all very well for an expert trader. That is true, but I am merely illustrating the difference between what the public regards as the most desirable objective and the possibilities which lie ahead for the trader who gains knowledge and experience and becomes adept at trading.

These opportunities are constantly presented by the market's fluctuations. Follow those in Telephone along until the end of April, 1933, and you find that in the eleven months' period they total 363 points without going out of the range 71–121. This is the equivalent of a rise from 71 to 434 if all these 5 point moves were added together.

In the final analysis, the rise of 50 points was less than one-eighth of the total movements of 5 points or more.

Stock Market Opinions

"WHAT do you think of the market?" is a standard form of greeting in Wall Street. Of all foolish questions this is the worst.

It would take hours to answer that question properly, and before the time was up I'd have to begin all over again, because my opinion would have changed in many respects, with the market. Questioners seem to know this unconsciously; for they are usually content with any sort of answer. I've tried this out by replying on various occasions: "Strong." "Rotten." "Dead." "Haven't seen it lately." "What do you think?" Of course none of these comments really answers the question; but "they satisfy" — especially the last, which gives the inquirer an opportunity to air his own views without listening to mine.

Suppose one should take this ambiguous question seriously: It will put no money into his pocket to hear my opinion of the stock market as an economic institution, or to learn my emotional reactions to its behavior. Then what does the query mean, and how can it be answered? It will improve your trading methods to think this out carefully.

Make it personal. You mean to ask: "What do you think the market is going to do?" You wish me to forecast for you, and make it snappy. This clears the atmosphere some, but the question is still hazy. Do you want to know what the market is going to do in the next hour or two, or during the next few days, or weeks, or months, or years? Are you asking how far the next move will go, and how long it will last? If so, which move — the short, medium, or long swing? Do you refer to the averages, or to your especial pet stocks? If I'm to make the answer snappy you must be specific as to these points.

Even then I can not answer the inquiry satisfactorily until I know something about your financial condition and your method of operating. Are you a scalper of fractions? Do you trade for the longer swings? Or are you an investor, seeking only an income from interest and dividends? What is your present market position — in detail?

Even with all this information I'm still reluctant to answer your question without knowing whether you will follow my advice. If so, am I expected to look you up and tell you when I change my opinion, or will you undertake to keep in close touch with me?

The facts are that the market has more than one trend at the same time. The short trend may be upward, with the longer swing downward. Moreover, some stocks may be headed for lower prices while others move forward. If you've just bought Steel at 50, intending to hold for a few years until the price doubles, why should I upset your plan by predicting a reaction in the stock? Suppose Steel does slip back to 40 temporarily and then mounts slowly and irregularly to 100: my forecast of the nearby movement would have been correct; but it may have scared you out of an ultimately profitable long-pull position. If I never saw you afterward, there would be no opportunity to suggest that you buy the stock back at the lower level. Years later, if the stock does hit 100, you will cuss me out for giving what (according to my trading methods) was really good advice.

Market forecasting is not only complicated, it should be made to apply to your individual situation. Advice which would fit in with my way of operating might throw your plan out of gear. Hence these widely sought market opinions carry a heavy responsibility to the giver, and may be worse than useless to the receiver.

Why not do your own forecasting?

Little Tricks and Tricksters

THE great Stock Market successes of the past have not been based on some little "patented" ideas like playing "heads and shoulders," or gaps, halfway points or double bottoms, or any of those horseshoe stunts that are supposed to yield profits.

I have stood over the same ticker with James R. Keene, John W. Gates, Jesse L. Livermore, and other big operators, and not one of them made their plays on any of these queer notions pursued by people who are looking for easy ways to beat the market.

What Keene, Gates and Livermore did that distinguished them from these piddling ways is simply this: *They used their judgment.* By constant and continuous practice in trading in the stock market over a long period of years, they were successful more often than not.

And that is all there is to this business of trading in stocks scientifically and successfully. You have to learn how to use your judgment.

Wall Street is full of people who have been thus wasting time around the tape for years and years. Some of them do make money at times, but they could accomplish this if they merely tossed pennies to see when they should buy or sell; or stuck a pin in the back of the stock list to see what they should trade in.

What anyone must do if he undertakes this business seriously is to learn the basic principles on which the market operates, and, unless he gets these clearly and thoroughly into his head, he better put his money into the savings bank. Once he has these principles imbedded where they can't get away, he can fill in all the other essentials provided he knows how and where to get them and learns properly to apply them.

TWENTY FOUR

A few years ago the woods were full of people who were willing to tell others what to buy and sell and when. The advisory profession as a means of extracting money from the gullible, having been fully exploded at least to this generation in the past four years, many soothsayers are now flocking into the business of teaching others how to trade. The fact that they have never made any big money themselves is no obstacle to their claiming that they are now "authorities." Each has a "staff of technicians." Their knowledge dates back to the days when Dan Drew was selling cattle and learning the game himself. Their synthetic effusions overflow endless books, pamphlets, circulars and what-nots.

In the midst of this welter we should recall the fact that water never rises higher than its source, and that stealing other people's ideas and putting them out as your own will not lead to any permanent success.

The proof of a man's ability to teach others is this: Has he ever made any big money in the market for himself or for others, on the basis of his judgment?

I have found a very good way of testing the ability of those who claim they can forecast or show you how. It is this: Ask them to send you a postal card after the close or before the opening on any day when they have predictions or advice to submit. The postmark will show when it was mailed, and time will tell whether it would have yielded a profit. Thus both of you will know the facts. As a result of this test, I have found that 99.44 percent soon drop out of the prediction business.

A similar procedure might be adopted for those who claim to be "experts" and "authorities." Ask them to prove by documentary evidence how, when and where they got to be experts and authorities. If truthful, they can prove it. Put it up to them. If you swallow their arguments whole all of them will appear to stand at the head of their profession. Make 'em come across.

Astrology and the Stock Market

IN HIS class at the New School of Social Research in New York City, Professor Irving J. Saxl, in response to a question from a student on Thursday evening, November 29, 1933, stated: "Within the last three years there has been a systematic attempt to check up on the accuracy of predictions made by a number of astrologers, by a Society formed for that purpose. It was found in 85% of the predictions made and analyzed, these predictions did not come true."

Many people have endeavored to forecast the stock market by this means. Prominent astrologers have claimed that the late J. P. Morgan and other large banking interests have consulted them frequently. We are wondering whether the astrologers of twenty years ago were any more accurate than those now employing this means of forecasting.

Every so often someone claims that he can produce marvelous results by astrology, but we have never heard of anyone becoming hopelessly rich in this way. Nevertheless (as quoted from Professor Saxl), it is estimated that Americans pay $25,000,000 annually for horoscopes, fortune-telling, reading tea leaves, etc. This indicates what a hold this subject has on the public.

We do not say there is nothing in astrology, for as everyone will admit, *sometimes such predictions come true*. But until the record above mentioned became known, there was no definite or very scientific checkup on the net result. It is the *net* that counts.

Perhaps for one who has his head so far up in the clouds, it is a pardonable error to forecast stock market price movements on New Year's day. But what apology may the author of the following forecast offer for the rest of his dire January predictions?

An Object Lesson in Astrology

| WHAT THE STARS FORETOLD (?) | WHAT THE MARKET REALLY DID |

WHAT THE STARS FORETOLD (?)

"Market Forecast for January, 1934" as taken from the magazine, *American Astrology* for that month.

In our September issue, published August 25, we stated that in our opinion the high point of the year had not been reached, which implied that we expected the market to average above the July peak before the end of the year.

WHAT THE MARKET REALLY DID

As recorded by the *New York Times*. Average of 50 stocks.

	High	Low
July, 1933	98.05	76.53
Aug., 1933	93.79	80.40
Sept.,1933	92.76	79.15
Oct., 1933	85.62	71.91
Nov., 1933	86.83	74.81
Dec., 1933	89.04	80.54

We shall expect if anything new advances between December 31 and January 8. Following January 8, we pass the zone of safety. It is possible, in fact highly probable, that the market may continue to push upward to the 15th, but after January 8 it is a false market. . . . Those who KNOW what it is all about will step out not later than January 13.

Dec.	30	86.02	
Jan.	2	86.99	
Jan.	3	86.03	
Jan.	4	84.69	
Jan.	5	84.78	
Jan.	6	83.59	
Jan.	8	84.00	82.77
Jan.	13	85.70	84.64
Jan. 8 to 13		86.69	82.77

The week of January 15 is likely to be disastrous to many people. . . . During that week we shall expect the market to be depressed in a very decided fashion. The break may come on any one of two days, viz.: January 15 or 17. In any case the wise investor will be out and off on the side lines not later than Saturday, January 13.

Jan.	15	89.99	86.32
Jan.	16	91.80	89.59
Jan.	17	92.02	89.93

DAILY INDICATIONS

Jan. 1. Up and Down — up *then* down. Opens with good intentions. A day of violent reactions, but develops reactionary tendencies toward the close.

New Year's Day—Holiday

Jan. 2. This looks like a battle between the Bulls and the Bears — the Bears triumph. Short selling forces the market down under considerable pressure.

High	Low	Last
86.99	85.41	85.83

Jan. 3. Those who sold short yesterday should have no difficulty delivering on today's prices. A pessimistic day.

86.03 83.95 84.61

Jan. 4. Here is where the market finds solid footing again and prepares for new advances. Trend of the day — upward.

84.69 82.77 84.27

Jan. 5. This should be a busy day. Prices should advance to a marked extent. Volume large — closes strong.

84.78 83.09 83.42

Jan. 6. Advance continues, market shows much strength. Closes strong.

83.59 82.86 83.17

Jan. 8. Profit taking cuts heavily into any gains there may be. Large turnover. Closes steady with moderate losses. . .

84.00 82.77 83.02

Jan. 9. Traders are in a buying mood today. Strongly speculative, optimistic.

84.64 83.42 83.92

Jan. 10. Opens strong. Closes weak.

86.06 84.21 85.90

Jan. 11. A bull market appears to be just about at the top for this rise and is hesitating on the verge of a break.

86.69 85.30 86.14

Jan. 12. Probably quite active, but heavy profit taking may hold any tendency there is to advance. Net result — price change may be slight.

Jan. 13. Sell.

86.62 85.18 85.57
85.70 84.64 85.37

Jan. 15. This is the day when the foundations may suddenly slide away and bring the entire price structure crashing downward.	89.99	86.32	89.75
Jan. 16. The above situation is likely to continue throughout the week. . . . Downward trend continues.	91.80	89.59	90.65
Jan. 17. Some more sad news. Looks as though the market is receiving a pretty thorough purging, although the general tone is much less pessimistic. . .	92.02	89.93	90.74
Jan. 18. Pessimistic. The market is in a cynical mood and goes fishing for an anchorage again, looks though it might go pretty deep, but it will also find the bottom today.	91.54	89.99	90.44
Jan. 19. This date should mark the turning point and the commencement of a new advance — BUY.	93.44	91.98	92.20

His position on the long side lasted till January 27, when the instructions were: "Might be a good idea to temporarily unload today."

From all of the above we conclude that these predictions have about borne out the average of "85% wrong" mentioned by Professor Saxl. Perhaps the Editor of *American Astrology* should consult a numerologist or a palmist. We hope that his readers did not take too seriously the "most dangerous, destructive and utterly disastrous configuration of the planets that we have found in many months" for the January 15 to January 22 "storm center."

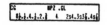

Traders I Have Known

Third Prize Story in Our Recent Contest

WHEN I went into the market, a year or so ago, it was against the advice of those well-wishing friends who always rally to the support of those washed up on the shores of inactivity by the depression. This was also against the ideas of my immediate family, members of which opined that marketeering was a low form of gambling. However six customers' men also assured me that I was ordained to be a big operator, and that settled the matter. Someone dropped a sage remark that ninety-five percent of the public is always wrong. I determined to put reverse English on the usual proceedure — try to learn what *not* to do and how not to do it. This obituary would apply to most traders I have met:

> The body that lies here was Johnny O'Toole's —
> He played the Big Board without knowing the rules.

Johnston A. O'Toole drifted into the boardroom with a wad of currency in his hand and an idea in his head. His wife was a swell dreamer and she had just come out of a trance, wherein her grandmother had shown her a picture of Uncle Sam's battle cruisers passing in formation. Johnny spent a day trying to find a stock to fit that picture, and when I whimsically suggested NAV as filling the naval requirement, he right away bought a hundred shares. A few days later NAV went ex-dividend and Johnny found himself with a hundred shares of Sperry Corp., which shortly afterward he sold at 3¾, washed up his original purchase at a profit. Mister O'Toole was by now a seasoned and successful trader.

The next dream was a puzzler. Mrs. O'Toole was all hot and bothered after dreaming of a short length of rope.

Again my happy faculty for reading 'em was called upon, and what more natural than the sale of the stock of a company making cigars? Rope did I say? Anyway, Johnny went short a hundred, around twenty-three — and climbed hastily out ten points higher, at the urgent request of the broker's margin clerk. But that was just the beginning.

Next wifie called to John, early one morning in July, that she had had a vivid dream of a soldierly figure done in brass or bronze. So he scanned the "600" and decided that General Bronze filled the bill. The stock was cheap at $8\frac{1}{2}$ and Johnny took on three hundred, thinly margined. The going was great until the July cyclone took him out of the market — again at the insistence of the same hard-boiled margin chaser who didn't believe in dreams. John hasn't been seen since.

Please do not think I'm judging the other fellow's operations through a pair of spectacles that I'm ashamed to look through myself. I've made more mistakes than the average trader, and I cheerfully admit it. But on with the story.

Reserve a place of honor for old Ed Gager — the man who was never licked. Once he made up his mind as to what the "big fellows" were going to do, he *knew*, and he'd stay put until all hell froze. Ed was bullish in the spring, and cashed in on the inflation boom to the tune of $4,000 in Bond and Share, and several more in Baldwin, Belding Hemingway, *et al*. He got out before the mid-summer break, and the customer's men pointed him out to embryonic operators as the farmer who came to town and showed Wall Street a thing or two. I wish the tale could stop there, but not so. Ed turned bearish on September 9 with the Dow Jones averages at 99, and sold an armful of this and that. He was right, he didn't care who knew it, and "they" couldn't fool *him*. A glance at your chart will show what happened. Anyway, he watched them go up against him, for ten days, and on the 19th closed out his line at the 105 level, where he was positive stocks were headed for 125. And he was positive enough to load up with three or four good ones — not so many as the last lot, it's true, because the exchequer was slightly warped. Among them, he rode his long Locomotive down to the early twenties, where he switched over to the short side again, still absolutely sure that he was right. I looked for Ed yesterday, and they said that he had gone back to the farm for a rest.

Then there was Billy Mathews, a dope-sheet fiend. In his collection he had one or more of every analytical survey, market forecast and Wall Street Barometer that easy running printing presses have turned out since Adam forecasted trouble in EVE Preferred. By referring to a chart of thirty-seven stocks, which he carried in a vest-pocket edition, done in tooled leather, he could tell you what the Governor of North Carolina said to President Whitney of the Exchange — and why. Billy developed quite a following in the happy days of May and June, when the market was climbing, and he got out on the 7th of July, in line with instructions and according to Chart Number 81. But he bought clear up to the legal limit at the close of that first day of the decline, and you will remember that there were two more heavy selling days after that. He hasn't been the same Bill since, but he has reduced the number of his "services." He told me he is now taking only an even dozen.

One more name for the marble slab, and I am through. Doc. Andrea was a dentist in the suburbs with a nice practice. Early in '29, thirty thousand ducats fell into his lap, through the sudden demise of a provident relative. Doc. "invested" the whole mess in the market in September of that historic year and it went through in fine shape. They left him with a 22 carat filling in the third frontal bicuspid.

Doc. was sure it was all a mistake, so back he came in

'33 with some brand-new bills and a world of rosy optimism. Doc's trading always reminded me of those cornhusk beds they have out in Ioway: one minute you're in, and the next minute you're out. He would ask every responsive soul in the room for advice, buy something that struck his fancy, then immediately go sour on his deal. He just *knew* he shouldn't have bought that. Usually his revised opinion was right. However, his happy smile and friendly chatter brightens up a dull day in the boardroom, but as his broker said awhile ago, "If you want to make money, find out what Doc. Andrea is doing, and do the opposite."

Doc. is still with us, but I hear his office girl calling him back to finish an inlay, started last Michaelmas.

> You can growl at the gang down in Wall Street
>   When you're caught with your tail in a crack;
> You can call 'em pet names 'till you're dizzy,
>   But that won't bring lost dollars back.
>
> Before you go into the next scrimmage,
>   Remember you alone are to blame —
> If you don't take a leaf from their notebook,
>   And study the rules of the game.

My greatest successes have been ascribed merely to good fortune; and my reverses will no doubt be imputed to my faults. But if I should write an account, it will be seen that, in both cases, my reason and faculties were exercised in conformity with principles.

* * *

If we were always to wait for the most favourable combination of circumstances, no enterprise would ever be undertaken. There can be no end without a beginning — there never was an enterprise in which everything fitted in perfectly, for chance plays a leading part in all the affairs of men. Obedience to rule does not ensure success, but success on the other hand furnishes a canon — a rule of conduct. — *Napoleon.*

Annuities—The Foundation of Financial Independence

This department is conducted by David A. Lunden-Moore.

AN OLD French saying: "The institution of life insurance is a marvelous structure: mathematics laid the foundation and character built the roof."

Annuities are sold by life insurance companies under a guarantee to pay the purchaser a stipulated income for life. The income never fluctuates. It is paid regularly on any date fixed by the Annuitant. The return from an Annuity depends upon age. The older you are the larger the return.

The various types of Annuities provide this guaranteed income either to one person or to several.

Annuities can be purchased in a lump sum or in installments.

The proceeds from an Annuity are free from Federal Tax for a considerable number of years. There is no better way to secure safety and regularity of income. When you purchase an Annuity you buy financial freedom. Happiness and security are inseparable companions. Financial independence means security.

For centuries the people of Great Britain, France and Holland, where conservative investments are the rule and not the exception, have looked upon Annuities as the most sacred of trusts. And in our country we have yet to find the man or woman who has ever failed to receive an Annuity check when due. The reason for the safety and stability of Annuities can be found in the very nature of the institution of life insurance.

THE GREAT RESERVOIR

An insurance company is like a great reservoir. Millions of policyholders and Annuitants pay their premiums monthly, quarterly, or annually. Day in and day out the vast flow of money runs into the great reservoir. Trained Actuaries (expert mathematicians), together with skilled financial experts, under the guidance of the strictest State supervision, keep a steady watch over the reservoir. Every move is strictly calculated.

The law of averages functions with the same precision as the motion of the planets. Year after year the liabilities of our great life insurance companies are calculated with painstaking care, and a factor of safety is always added to make conditions doubly sure.

For almost a century our life insurance companies have been discharging their obligations to a steadily increasing army of Annuitants. Civil war, financial panics, epidemics, the World War and the present depression have never interfered with the institution of life insurance. In the last five years payments by life insurance companies amounted to over thirteen billion dollars. The great reservoir is always there, ready to distribute benefits and income among those who belong to the vast army of over sixty million policyholders and Annuitants in the United States.

What the Annuity can do for you, and its place in your investment program, is illustrated in a chart which we shall be glad to send you on request. The charts have been prepared at considerable expense; we therefore reserve the right to distribute them at our discretion.

LETTERS FROM ANNUITANTS

"Feeling the need of an increase in income, and desiring to eliminate risk of loss through reinvestment or through other causes, I conceived the idea, in the year 1902, of investing in Annuities. After taking my first Annuity, I never doubted its wisdom. I therefore continued my purchases regularly, every 18 months taking out one until I had 16 in 1928. The benefits totaled $10,000 per year, in quarterly payments. The 100 instalments have been regularly received, not one a day late. Aggregate receipts to date amount to about $125,000. I made it a rule to apply a certain amount of the receipts (whatever I could spare) to the purchase of additional Annuities. I am now in my 90th year." — *C. P. C., Brooklyn, New York.*

"My wife and I are elderly people. Some years ago we decided to put our savings into Annuities. It is very comfortable in times like these to have these amounts coming in. I have advised my friends and clients similarly situated that an Annuity is the very best form of provision for old age. It is not very difficult for an industrious and thrifty person to earn and save money, but *to keep it safely* after it has been saved is outside of the experience of nine such persons out of ten. A man puts money in the savings bank and he is under a constant temptation to spend it for immediate pleasures, and he is always liable to be the victim of persons who try to induce him to make some unwise investment involving usually the loss of his money." — *A. A. H., New York City.*

ANNUITY CHECKS GOOD IN ITALY

"In regard to our Joint Annuity I can say that when we remember our former worries with defaulted interest and passed dividends, we feel more than compensated for the loss incurred by selling securities on a falling market. The excellent return and the prompt arrival of checks give us peace of mind. Also in nearly every letter from Italy my sister, who is an Annuitant, expresses her satisfaction in her Annuity. Her serenity during the bank holiday was in great contrast to the panic of most of her American friends in Rome. It was of vital importance for us to find an investment providing for the security of the future." — *H. B. B., Bennington, Vt.*

CERTAINTY OF RETURN FOR LIFE ONLY THROUGH ANNUITY

"I took out my first Annuity in 1923 to 'get the feel of it.' I was then only 57 and was doubtful of the wisdom of parting with money, turning it over entirely to life insurance companies to manage and pay me annually as long as I should live, an agreed amount. The experience was comforting and altogether satisfactory. I never questioned the certainty of the payments, and they have always arrived on time. The yield has been greater than could be secured from any other form of investment at all comparable in safety. I have recommended an Annuity to a friend within two days." — *A. M. H., Beverly Hills, Cal.*

PUT MONEY INTO ANNUITIES LARGELY TO PROTECT WIFE

"Since I retired from business thirteen years ago I have put a large amount of money into Joint Annuities, largely to protect my wife in possible event of anything happening to me. We have found Annuities of more value even than we expected, especially during the past four years. I am the envy of a host of intimates because I have had a real income. It seems to me that every man who has any money after reaching middle age, and especially later, owes it to himself to invest in Annuities." — *H. L. A., New York City.*

High Spots
In a Wall Street Career

This condensed series is from Mr. Wyckoff's autobiography "Wall Street Ventures and Adventures Through 40 years." It will be continued through several more issues.

1905 Studying the Big Fellows—*Continued*

GEORGE A. KESSLER'S agency for White Seal Champagne netted him 50 cents on every bottle sold in the U. S., or some $500,000 a year. This enabled him to play in stocks with some of the big boys. He came one day to Wasserman's office, and instead of sitting down at the little low ticker as usual, went in behind the order desk and watched the tall ticker there. When he had been there about an hour and a half, he then came out, saying to Wasserman: "Well, Eddie, I have just bought the last twenty thousand shares of Tennessee Coal and Iron necessary to give our crowd control of the company. And if any of you fellows will buy it now at $125 and put it away for a year, you will get $250 for it."

Said Major Armstrong, "Your buying has already put it up several points. We don't want anything we've got to hang on to for a year. Give us something for a quick turn." Kessler only smiled at that and a few minutes later left the office. (Some months later, T. C. & I. sold well above $160.)

The next day Wasserman handed me a fat bundle of stock certificates. "Here's the twenty thousand Tennessee Coal that Kessler bought yesterday," he said. "Will you take it to Moore & Schley and get a check?" I put the certificates in a portfolio, walked up Broadway to No. 80, passed the bundle into the delivery window in Moore & Schley's office, and received in return a check for something over $2,000,000, which their bank promptly certified for me.

Moore & Schley were the bankers for the pool. It was the tremendous load of T. C. & I. they were carrying for the pool in several New York banks that was to play such a large part in the failure of some of these institutions two years later, in the panic of 1907. At that time, with the panic at its worst, it became evident that unless these banks were relieved of their Tennessee Coal loans, more big bank failures would follow, and many brokerage house failures. The Steel Corporation was willing to take over all of this Tennessee Coal and give in exchange therefor its 5% bonds, which would be good collateral. This was at the height of the Trust-Busting days, but J. P. Morgan and E. H. Gary went to Washington, explained the situation to President Roosevelt and asked whether, if this were done, the Steel Corporation would be subjected to further prosecution by the government on the ground that it was establishing a monopoly. The President promised that no action would be taken by the government if the situation were thus relieved. The transaction was immediately effected: the Tennessee Coal in the banks was all exchanged for U. S. Steel bonds, and the pool found itself again in a liquid condition.

* * *

A very amusing person, this Edward Wasserman, quite a big trader. When he was long of the market, and it was going up, he bellowed like a bull all over the place. Each succeeding advance in the price of his stock was announced in stentorian tones. But when the market crashed and he was either long, or out of it, he would pussy-foot up and down the big office, behind the curved window[1] where the ticker was located, and ask everyone in a thoroughly scared stage whisper: "Do you think there's going to be a panic?"

One day when he was short of about 10,000 shares of Steel, he, his brother Jesse, his friend, M. A. Bernheimer, and I were sitting around the ticker. The day was hot; Eddie went into the shower he had had installed in his private office. While he was taking his bath some one called to him that Steel had just broken a few points. Without a strip of clothing, waving a Turkish towel in one hand, Eddie pranced right into the customer's room. "How is it now?" he yelled. "Anything on the news ticker?"

"Go back, you damned fool," cried his brother Jesse, "all Broadway can see you!"

At noon he would order lunch from Rohrer's Restaurant in the basement and whoever happened to be in the office at the time would be invited. He selected queer combinations of food. One day, after Eddie had ordered, Dick Canfield came in, and was

[1] Now part of Hornblower & Weeks' front office.

invited. The waiter served the main course — pigs' feet and sauer-kraut. On a side table he set the dessert — plum pudding.

"Pigs' feet, sauerkraut and plum pudding!" Canfield exclaimed. "For God's sake, Eddie, let a gentleman order the luncheon after this!"

Many of Wasserman's campaigns were started out of thin air. One day when the tape was barely moving, he said to the clients in the office: "Let's make up a little pool in Southern Railway and start a move in it. I'll buy a thousand if you will."

Eddie went over on the floor and bought a few thousand shares all at one price. "It came easily," he said. Then he called up friends and told them there was going to be a move in Southern Railway. When all these trades appeared on the tape in such an absolutely dead market, it did look as though something had started. Here was a chance for some of the thousands of people sitting around hundreds of tickers all over the country to get a little action. Out-side buying orders began to come into the crowd; in a few minutes Southern Railway was up a point and a half. Eddie and his friends quickly took their profits. The evening papers said Morgan had been buying Southern Railway.

*   *   *

Being curious as to the details of the floor trader's point of view, I had a talk about that time with Isaac N. Spiegelberg, who made his headquarters in our office. He had no clients; he simply stood at one of the posts on the floor all day and bought and sold for his own account. I learned that his yearly earnings had averaged in the hundred thousands for some years.

Spiegelberg told me that he had started doing a regular broker-age business on the floor and that he would have been "at it yet" had he not, one day, executed an order in the wrong stock. Instead of cutting his loss short as soon as he discovered his mistake, he had let it run and finally had got into a bad hole. He had decided that there was too much risk in proportion to the small class of business, so he decided to become a floor trader, and leaving out the first few years of apprenticeship, he had made money at this ever since.

His method was to select one of the most active stocks and stay in that crowd day after day, familiarizing himself with the peculiar-ities of its movements and getting an insight into the manipulation of it. Constant observation showed him that his success or failure depended largely on his ability to follow the immediate trend, and to turn quickly if he was wrong. But he explained that the most important thing in floor trading is to cut your losses short and go with the stock as long as it travels your way. The most accurate guide, he claimed, was the tendency and the technical position of the market.

I asked him whether he ever took a position in the market (that is, took on a line of stocks for a few weeks or months). He answered: "Occasionally I take a position, but whenever it bothers me in my trading I close it out. At one time I got long of Reading before it fell into a slump and when my loss ran into $25,000 I let it go because I found I couldn't judge the other stock in which I was also trading, if I had to be running over to the Reading post all the time."

Losses such as this did not bother him much. I once heard Wasserman ask him after the day's close how he had come out. He said: "Oh! I got fooling with this Smelters, found myself on the wrong side, took my loss, and finally got a position at the bottom; then I bought some more on the way up, and began to get a profit. But I was too impatient. I sold it out, and then it went up four or five points more."

"How much did you make?" Eddie inquired.

"Only about ninety-seven hundred," Ike replied ruefully, "if I hadn't been in such a hurry I would have had a good day."

* * *

Carsten Boe, who often visited Wasserman to find out what campaign the latter might be planning, got out a market letter. This letter at one time had been quite successful, but unfortunately, after all his bull campaigns, Boe had once turned bearish — and had lost most of his subscribers. They were willing to pay him for advice when it was bullish; they dropped him like a hot potato when he turned bear.

"I vill never pe pearish again," he would wail.

* * *

I had now spent the greater part of seventeen years in Wall Street — as a boy, clerk, silent partner and managing partner in Stock Exchange houses. But with all I had seen, studied and observed, I had yet no well-defined plan or method for money-making in the stock market, either for my clients or for myself. Like every other trader and investor, I had had profits and suffered losses; what few notes I have of my early trading indicate that my strongest asset was my determination to keep losses down. Never risking more than a small part of my capital, I did not lose any big money in the market, even though the term "big" be used in proportion to the capital employed. My commitments were seldom over 500 or 1,000 shares. Just as much could be learned from dealing in hundred-share lots as from larger amounts, and my records were kept with a view to showing progress made toward having more net points profit than points loss. By comparing the results of different trading periods I could judge whether or not I was advancing.

Like most stock brokers and customers' men, I had found it difficult to concentrate upon the problem of forecasting the market, difficult to do any material amount of deep research. I was faced with the constant example of wrong methods used by clients and resulting in losses. They would insist on overtrading. They would want to use $1,000 to margin two or three hundred shares, whereas with their inexperience and limited capital they should have been trading only in twenty-five or fifty shares.

Clients persisted in buying only when the market was strong; and seldom on reactions, and without any regard for general or technical conditions. Also they would sell out on the weak spots, reversing the rule of the Rothschilds who bought "sheep" and sold "deer." Many formed the expensive habit of jumping in and out of the market so actively that commissions would eat them up — they paid too much money into the kitty. This practice was good for my commission account, but it killed them off.

One small trader opened an account with $1,000 and bought and sold so frequently that although he was a fair judge of the market and often guessed right, he finally was down to trading in ten shares and was then wiped out. Analyzing the record of his transactions, I found that he had paid $3,000 in commissions while in the process of losing his $1,000. In other words, he had paid in commissions his $1,000 capital and $2,000 he had made in the market.

Most of those who dealt in our office, in spite of all I could do, would take small profits but would let their losses run until they were broke, tied up or crippled. They seemed to apply the rules that they used in their own businesses, rather than those demanded by the peculiar and technical requirements of successful stock market speculation.

At Wasserman's I was having a better chance. I had more time to give to analysis of the market; I could concentrate on this subject with less interference; there were private offices equipped with tickers where I could study the action of prices without interruption for half an hour or so at a time. Studying my records I found that I was obtaining improving results.

I wanted to find out whether it was possible to develop a judgment that was reliable in the *majority* of cases, never for a moment entertaining the idea that I could be right all the time. My greatest problem was to eliminate emotion—to learn to trade with a poised mind, without fear or hope. Whenever a stock went in my favor or against me, and I found myself still unbiased in my "feelings," I was much encouraged. What I wanted was to acquire a trained judgment, combined with the experience that comes only from constant practice.

Other installments will follow

Stock Market Regulation

An Appraisal of Its Possible Effects
on Traders and Investors

(The answers allow for the possibility of the bill being passed in most drastic form. Latest information points to favorable modifications which would, of course, strengthen the conclusions set forth.)

1. Q. Will regulation require change in technique of stock trading?

A. Before we undertake to answer this question, let us first consider the nature of the problem with which the investor and trader have to deal. Both will concede that advancing security prices are based upon the expectation and ultimate realization of rising corporate earnings. Falling prices, i.e. bear markets, begin with the expectation of declining earnings and the fall of prices continues so long as corporate profits persist in their downward course.

However, an advance in the price level, of itself, is not produced by the actual or prospective improvement in earnings. These are simply the motivating influences which create an increasing demand for stocks. That is, either the knowledge or belief that earnings may increase is sufficient to stimulate the desire for stocks and buyers express this desire in the form of orders to purchase. Those who already hold securities, meanwhile, become less and less willing to sell. Thus it is that demand expands, supply falls off and prices advance. The rise in prices will continue, moreover, just as long as the force of demand is greater than the supply. We then have the phenomenon known as a "bull" market and, of course, a "bear" market is initiated and continued by the reverse of these conditions.

A host of modifying, abetting or contradictory influences may come into play during the development of either a bull or bear cycle. Some of these factors may be political, some manipulative, others purely technical. All are reflected in the changing forces of demand and supply. It is for this reason that experienced traders and investors prefer to reduce the problem of what, and when, to buy and sell to its simplest terms by employing technique, that is, the method of analyzing manifestations peculiar to the law of demand and supply.

This brings us to the question whether demand or supply, or both, may be affected by regulation of the stock exchanges. As we shall see later, there is a possibility that the supply of certain types of stocks might be increased temporarily, and certain manipulative maneuvers may be modified. But it is apparent that sound basic principles of analyzing supply and demand must remain as effective as ever. This is especially true when we consider that rising and falling corporate profits are the fundamental motivating causes of the urge to buy or sell. Congress has manifested no intention of seeking to control the economic cycle, through stock regulation, even though opponents of the proposed legislation contend, with no little justification, that the original bill would permit disturbing governmental interference with business.

2. Q. Will it increase or decrease activity?

A. There is room for much difference of opinion on this point. A great deal depends upon the form legislation may take at its final passage through Congress. Uncertainty on this point has already been productive of restraint on the part of many traders. It may be contended that the removal of this uncertainty would, of itself, act with tonic effect on the market's activity.

Margin requirements, if applied on the basis of the original draft of the bill, would curtail the activities of the average small trader. Under present margin requirements, accounts with debit balances of less than $5,000 must have a margin equivalent to 50% of the debit balance. Thus, an individual with $1,000 capital may purchase 100 shares of a stock selling at $30, since his debit balance would be $2,000 and his initial $1,000 deposit would be 50% of the amount borrowed from his broker. But if he be required to post 60% of the market price of this same stock, he could carry but 55 shares. There is an alternative proposal in the original version of the bill, that a buyer may borrow 80% of the lowest price at which a stock sold in the preceding three years. But these "lowest prices" in most instances are too far removed from existing quotations to materially influence the net effect of the 60% proposal.

We must assume, therefore, that many traders would be com≡ pelled to trade in fewer shares so that the daily volume of transactions would be correspondingly reduced. There are certain compensating factors, however, which would be likely to modify this result. For one thing, if stock prices were to rise, stockholders' equities would also expand and their purchasing power must therefore also gain.

Secondly, the ordinary buyer has a marked prejudice against "high-priced" stocks. He does not trade in them extensively as a rule, but gives preference to medium and low priced issues. Stiff margin regulations would simply strengthen this prejudice. Moreover, it must be remembered that most brokers already require that low priced stocks be purchased outright. That portion of the public which has been accustomed to deal in low priced stocks will thus gain new recruits. No one who is familiar with the American mind will be so rash as to suppose that the urge to speculate in securities may die. The only thing which could destroy speculation would be an economic system which might completely eliminate price fluctuations and hence remove the incentive to trade for profits. Man's ingenuity has yet to devise such a condition. Certainly it cannot be done by law. Surely it would be undesirable, even if it could be done, for such a condition would greatly temper, if not entirely destroy the incentive to participate in the industrial developments on which our welfare and high standards of living are founded. Drastic margins will simply induce the public to shift its operations from stocks in the higher priced brackets to those in the lower.

Lastly, there must also be considered the probable increase in activity which may flow from the reasons discussed in Question 3.

3. Q. Will it make common stocks more desirable or less desirable for investment: or more desirable or less desirable for speculation?

A. Except for the qualifying arguments considered in Questions 2 and 4, there is little ground for believing that the investment desirability of common stocks will be affected. The investor's primary desire is to obtain a reasonable income return on his principal. The profit motive exists, but is secondary. In other words, the investor does not buy with the idea of realizing profits from price fluctuations though, if he is prudent, he will aim to secure appreciation in value of his principal by entering the market at the bottom of major and intermediate cycles in the price movement, and selling at or near the tops of those movements.

No investor may view the prospect of drastic regulation with equanimity. But if the possibilities of reasonable regulation should be realized, the psychological effect might well be to increase the demand for common stocks as investments since the public may feel that the market has been purged of past abuses and might even regard regulation as in the nature of a governmental stamp of approval on the market. In any event, no attempt is being made to abolish economic cycles, which are the basic cause of long term price movements.

The original bill, for instance, makes no reference to control of economic cycles in its title, but states that "The national credit and the safety and stability of investment are intimately related to and affected by the prices for which securities are sold and offered for sale upon exchanges."

The original title further declares that "Regulation . . . is imperative in the public interest for the protection of interstate commerce, the national banking and Federal Reserve System." President Roosevelt himself has said, "It is my belief that exchanges for dealing in securities and commodities are necessary and of definite value to our commercial and agricultural life." Moreover, Senator Fletcher, one of the co-sponsors of the Stock Exchange bill, was quoted by the newspapers as stating that this legislation "is one of a series of steps to be taken for the purpose of bringing safety to the general public in the field of investment and finance."

Thus, it is a reasonable assumption that the administration has no deliberate intention of putting investors in strait-jackets, and those who invest intelligently should continue to find a satisfactory vehicle in common stocks.

With respect to intelligent speculation, the same general principles apply. But we must recognize the probable effects of undue restrictions on activity that are likely to make the market for stocks thinner; that is to say, reduce the total volume of transactions to an extent that will make prices jump over wider price intervals between sales owing to a reduction in immediate volume of supply and demand from hour to hour. Manifestly, a thinner market would increase the risks in short-swing trading because orders to buy or sell "at the market" could not in all probability be executed as close to the last sale as they would be if bids and offerings were more numerous and consequently closer to each other.

All things considered, the general principles of technical analysis would operate as usual, but somewhat greater caution would be required in placing orders "at the market." It is probable that this would simply have the effect of developing a policy of giving more serious consideration to the use of limited orders in ordinary purely speculative operations.

4. Q. Will the market become more liquid or less liquid?

A. Any influence which tends to retard the free flow of transactions, or to reduce activity, must necessarily produce a proportionate reduction in the market's liquidity. Markets are made by the meeting of minds of buyers and sellers. Thus, in the stock market, no actual transaction takes place until a buyer and a seller have agreed on a price which is mutually satisfactory.

Let us assume that A has 100 shares of Steel which he desires to sell at 50 and that B is willing to buy 100 shares of the same stock but wishes to pay only 49½. If these two were the only individuals interested in making a trade in Steel, at the moment, the "market" in that stock would then stand "49½ Bid, 50 Asked." Now, assume that a third person, C, decided that he must sell 100 shares of Steel "at the market." Obviously the best price he could receive would be 49½, that is, the price which B is willing to pay, and his order would be executed at that figure. Then, if a fourth individual were to enter an order to "Buy 100 Steel at the market," his order would be executed at A's asked price, namely, 50. Therefore, the effect of these transactions would be to make the price jump one-half point between trades, that is, from 49½ to 50. Traders would then say that "there is a thin market in Steel."

NOTE. — Lack of space prevents including the complete text of this article in STOCK MARKET TECHNIQUE. However, the entire set of answers to the questions set forth in the advertisement on page 45 is available to those who return the coupon.

The Little Tailor Who Made a Fortune

WHEN I knew him he was a wizened little Jewish tailor. On occasions he came to the traders' room, but had little to say to anyone. His visits always coincided with a marked reaction or a rapid upward move in the market. After a few days of intense watching of the board, he disappeared for another interval.

A trader who had known the little man for many years stated that he had considerable property — all made in the stock market; that he salted away his profits in real estate and now owned, in the locality of his small tailor shop in Brooklyn, half a block of houses. A more unlikely-looking possessor of wealth from Wall Street trading would be difficult to imagine.

The story of his trading impressed me as unique. Years ago (it must have been in 1904) when Steel common was very low, he purchased 200 shares at $9.50 a share. Eventually certificates were issued in his name. Whether he paid the entire amount at the time or not I do not know, but when I met him he showed me one of his certificates. It looked extremely worn, held together as it was in several places by transparent mending tissue.

His method was simple: When he believed the time ripe for a reaction, he took the old certificates to the broker's office and left them on deposit with the cashier. He would then go short 200 shares of Steel, generally at the market, and patiently watch and wait for a break to some predetermined level. When the correct point, in his judgment, was reached he would cover his 200 shares thus concluding the transaction. The broker would return his old certificate, together with a check, often close to a thousand dollars. He thereupon returned to his tailor shop and waited for another similar opportunity.

His procedure on subsequent upturns would be the same. His selling and buying were always exactly 200 shares. Sometimes, but not often, a further quick bulge disturbed his plans, but he waited till, without a loss, he could extract his certificates.

When I first met this old trader, U. S. Steel was over $100 a share. Opportunities for his kind of trading were many, but the price to which the stock rose or fell did not disturb him in the least.

Thus he accumulated his wealth slowly, safely and conservatively. It was difficult for me to see how he could have improved on his method, for it seemed perfectly adapted to his character and temperament.

Lately I inquired about this old Jewish trader and his faded U. S. Steel certificates, and was told that he still has the same ones. He appears in his old haunts, but not quite so often. He must be very old now — probably 90.

E. T. C.

See Both Sides

IT MAY well be asked: "How long is the stock market going to be a difficult problem for most people?" The answer is: Just so long as the public continue their attempts to judge the market by fundamental statistics — commodity prices, carloadings, corporation earnings, balance sheets, and other "conditions"; just so long as they ignore what is essentially the Science of Stock Speculation.

While not in any sense an exact science, the stock market is, in the last analysis, a study in the forces which raise and lower prices, all of which are expressed in the Law of Supply and Demand, the only real fundamental factor.

The public must learn to see both sides of the market and "know when to get out as well as when to get in." It is perfectly absurd for either big or little operators to play the Wall Street game almost solely from the long side. If you doubt the preponderance of bulls, think how few speculators of large or small calibre were able to benefit by the enormous declines of those panic and depression years.

No One Wins What Others Lose

ASK any Washington politician: "Who wins what the public loses by trading in stocks?" Ten to one he will say it is the little group of wealthy insiders who rig the market. His answer would be dead wrong, for it confuses stock trading with gambling. But the belief is widely held, and explains much of the current prejudice against Wall Street.

In order to get at the facts, let me phrase the question more directly: Who makes what you lose? The correct answer is: No one.

To prove this, suppose you have $10,000 in cash, and that I own 100 shares of XYZ now quoted at $100 a share.

Each of us is worth $10,000 only my wealth is in marketable securities which are the equivalent of cash.

Now suppose that you buy my stock at $100 a share. Immediately after the transaction, each of us is still worth $10,000. Only my wealth now is in cash and yours in stock.

Next suppose that the stock declines to $50 a share while you hold it. At $50 a share, your stock is worth only $5,000. Your wealth has shrunk by $5,000. Meanwhile I still have the $10,000 in cash.

Finally, suppose I re-purchase your stock at $50 a share. Immediately after this transaction you have $5,000 in cash, but no stock. Evidently you have lost $5,000. But I am worth $5,000 in cash and $5,000 in stock; which is just what I was worth at the outset.

Clearly then, though you have lost $5,000 by trading in stocks (unskilfully), I have neither made nor lost a nickel.

The mystery as to what became of the $5,000 you lost is cleared up as soon as one realizes that the loss occurred while you held the stock — not at the time you bought it, nor at the time you sold it. It was purely an inventory loss.

The property went bad on your hands, which is another way of saying that "Paper losses are real losses."

On the other hand, I happened to be smart enough, or lucky enough, to get out of the stock before it crashed. This *saved* me from losing money; but I *made* nothing by unloading on you at a high price and buying the stock back at a lower price.

It will be easier to grasp this truth if we turn to the real estate field where the judgment is not clouded by prejudice. Let us say you purchase a house and lot at its fair market price of $10,000. After a period of years, the neighborhood deteriorates and you discover that this property is now worth only $5,000. You have lost $5,000 on the investment but who won what you lost? No one. Even a politician could see that.

When the market declines, everyone who owns stocks loses money. No one makes what others lose. When prices advance, everyone who holds stocks makes money. No one loses what others make.

The Power of an Idea

The most important thing in all life is an idea, and *an idea is born in a second.*

We should realize it, concentrate on it, use every effort to extract the idea's full value, for it often leaves us the next second never to return again.

A wise man advises us to write down every good idea, as it is born. There are not so many of them. Millions of men have had thoughts, conceptions, ideas that might have made them important in the world's history, and have never amounted to anything because, while the thought was born, nothing was done about it. — *Brisbane.*

Flashes

FAILURE is thinking in a rut.

Luck is a much overworked alibi.

Action and Reaction may be equal but who ever made any money out of that idea?

A sound idea is like a pebble thrown into a pool. The circles of its influence continually widen.

Foresight: The natural growth of a due understanding of the relevant facts of the past and the present, from which the future is presently to emerge.

The best protection against losses in stocks is not a safe deposit box but a judgment that approaches one hundred percent accuracy in knowing when to buy and sell.

Anyone can be lucky now and then, or even half the time; but persistent success is certain proof of ability. Persistent losses in the stock market are the evidence of poor judgment, bad technique, or both.

Great events ever depend upon but a single hair. The adroit man profits by everything, neglects nothing which can increase his chances; the less adroit, by sometimes disregarding a single chance, fails in everything.

A Record Nearly Perfect

FROM three thousand miles west of the Stock Exchange comes a record to prove that one need not be close to the ticker in New York to accomplish anything worth while and that there is proven value in charts, graphs and other similar guides to supplement a sound method of trading.

It is the accomplishment of a trader who might be regarded as yet a novice or amateur. His record sheds light on a point emphasized by experienced market operators; that is, how necessary it is to study and observe, and do everything else helpful before risking real money.

Above all it shows how it is possible to take out of the business of trading in stocks handsome returns and a striking percentage of profits. Records like this demonstrate the business is just like others — that success is possible. In the professions of law, engineering, medicine and others, some people are eminently and many satisfactorily successful.

It is so with stock trading. The record of this student is 97% successful. In 1932 he was "green" in the business of trading in stocks. By his own words you may see what happened. He says: "I began to study in June, 1932. I spent about a year in preparation before actually trading. The complete record of my trades from September 27, 1933 to February 15, 1934 shows gross profits of 243⅛ points and losses of 1¾ points."

Allowing approximately ¾ of a point against each trade to represent commissions, tax, interest and the "invisible eighth" — altogether 42 points, there remain approximately 200 points *net profit* on 55½ trades, or 3.6 points per round trip.

The record is one of the best — it shows 97% accuracy of judgment. If it comprised only a few transactions it would not be noteworthy. It is a continuous record covering a period of almost five months.

Average profits of less than 4 points indicate a tendency to take small profits. From one point of view it could be said that as the risk must have been from ½ to 3 points, the average profit is not in correct proportion. In venturing ½ to 3 points risk one might say he should have endeavored to realize 5 points and upward.

This does not invalidate the brilliancy of the record. It illustrates strikingly what may be done by an individual operating under a logical method regardless of time or distance from New York.

Stock	Number of Trades 100 sh. lots	Total Points Profit	Average Points Profit per Trade
Auburn.....................	10½	64⅜	6.13
Atchison...................	8	58⅝	7.328
Am. & For. Power..........	5	41¼	8.25
Western Union.............	5	20¼	4.05
United Aircraft.............	10	17¼	1.725
Case......................	4	13¼	3.31
New York Central*........	7	8⅛	1.16
Gen. Am. Trans............	1	5⅛	5.125
Nat. Biscuit...............	1	4¼	4.25
Del. & Hudson.............	1	2⅞	2.875
Pub. Serv. N. J.............	1	4¼	4.25
Cons. Gas.................	2	1⅞	.938
Total...................	55½	241½	4.35

*Of these two were losing trades — altogether 1¾ points.

The Market is like a Moving Picture

The stock market is like a moving-picture film on which every flash is different in some respect from those that precede and follow. By observing every detail that appears on a film one may study the action of the characters, read their purposes, and judge what they are likely to do when put to the test. Obviously, nothing like a cut and dried system can be applied to such a series of observations, but it is frequently possible to tell, early in a film, how the action will terminate, notwithstanding the efforts of the author to disguise his purpose and deceive his audience. So it is with manipulation as it appears on the tape.

Trader versus Insider

EVERYBODY, or almost everybody, wants to be an insider. A multitude of people who trade in stocks either occasionally or frequently yearn to be on the inside of information, as it is said. They envy directors, operators, specialists, pool managers, traders or others who they believe know what is going on, or what is to be done in this or that operation.

It is quite natural the average man should feel this way. The country has read illuminating tales of fabulous amounts "insiders" made in the last great bull market, and how some reaped millions unloading on an excited and gullible public. It has been shown how syndicates, with enormous banking credit, boosted prices unbelievably and while doing so were selling reams of long stocks and quantities of short contracts.

With their imaginations fired by the thought of how wonderful to be an "insider," millions of traders fain would ramble in that Elysian field. They would dismiss all hard labor of study and work and be free of all watchfulness. They would like to know precisely what is going on behind the scenes, so as to know exactly what to do.

In the first place, they should be reminded there is "many a slip 'twixt the cup and the lip," even for "insiders." For them "all is not gold that glitters." The real story of many an insider in 1929 is tragic. For instance, a partner of one of the biggest banking houses of Wall Street lost virtually his entire fortune of millions and, in going down, dragged along one of his most intimate friends. To prove to this friend innocence of intentional misleading, he submitted for examination every scrap of his intimate personal financial transactions and affairs. And this man is partner of a house commonly supposed to know about everything going on in the market. The house name makes the story incredible.

And this is not the only sad tale of an insider. There are many stories of the romance of making money on the inside — and horrible examples of the opposite results. However, it is not to be denied that insiders often have the better of the trader. The latter must exercise every whit of ingenuity to discern what is happening. Insiders are often off guard against the unexpected. The shrewd trader is ever on a sharp lookout. The trader remembers accidents can happen. He is prepared.

An insider may be handicapped by his own heavy commitments, while the moderate trader generally can jump at the first sign of trouble.

Again, there are insiders enjoying tremendous advantages. Recently, for example, a great corporation changed its method of monthly reporting. It now tells you of shipments that were made. Formerly it announced unfilled orders. Many technical reasons were given for the change. Nevertheless, a limited number still have knowledge of what is ahead. The public learns what has happened — or history. It is not unreasonable then to assume that this knowledge makes more sure the market commitments of those who might know. Under the new arrangements they may know of large booking of orders while the outsider is left to guess.

The insider and his advantages have always plagued the market. Of course someone necessarily must know earnings, special developments, big orders, big earnings and many other things long before they become public property — generally the officers of the corporation. Obviously they may act with greater certainty in their operations.

All of which means the trader must use every scientific means of detecting accumulation or distribution. He is handicapped against the sure knowledge of those who manage affairs. But he need not be hopelessly in ignorance if he will observe indices that often betray in market action what insiders are doing.

Old Timer Analyzes Some Market Letters

" A LOT of traders," declared Old Timer, "remind me of my roommate at college, whom we called 'Aimless Algy.' He always thought it easier to have someone else solve his problem. He had lost confidence in his own ability. If he ever did get the answer for himself, he felt it was incorrect. Other students got tired of pulling him through, so Algy began to use 'ponies.'

"To Algy, professors' lectures were just a jumble of words. He looked and listened, but nothing registered. After running an ordinary four-term course into its seventh year his father took him away. At home he bragged about completing a post-graduate course. He set up in business as Consulting Engineer. In the little burg where he began, people thought 'Aimless' was a wizard. I was hoping he would never build a dam, tunnel, bridge or anything else."

Obviously Old Timer was comparing "Aimless Algy" with those Traders who are forever dodging about the office in their search for tips, hunches and opinions, and nosing through the Advisory Letters and other dope. Also with other Algys sitting by, watching symbols and figures on the translux.

"I see your point, Old Timer," said I. "No doubt you mean the files of market letters in the Customers' Room correspond to the 'ponies' Algy used. And their writers no doubt have convinced someone they, too, are wizards."

"You get the idea exactly," responded Old Timer. "Out of curiosity I picked up a lot of market letters after I saw the gang poring over them. Just wanted to see what I would get out of the lot. Let's read a few and see how well they jibe.

"Here's one that tells us the market is apt to be erratic today, with a higher opening — that they advise their clients to get out on that strength. Here's another that says yesterday's reaction was a correction the market required, but the closing rally was the beginning of an advance which will take prices into new high ground. Here's one more that puts the last right back into reverse. This chap believes it would be too bad if selling breaks in the first hour today, because the market made a triple top in the last three sessions. That would indicate he is bearish, but his conclusion is that he would like the market better if it would go right on through those tops. In case it does, he says, one should get on for a quick rise of several points."

"All that dope," continued Old Timer, "bullish, bearish and contradictory, would have cost us a lot of money were we subscribers. Here's another letter, more or less involved and very carefully hedged, but it finally says the public is loaded with stocks and there is no basis for a sustained rise. So you see they mostly contradict each other and none of them seem to know where they're going. They are like poor 'Aimless Algy.' No wonder he flunked. Maybe his 'ponies' were to blame."

"How do you know," I inquired, "but that Algy is writing one of these stock market letters?"

A lawyer must understand the law and its interpretation before he is competent to draw a contract or try a case.

A navigator must understand how to determine his position at all times before he is competent to command an ocean liner.

The difference between the folk who do, and those who dream wistfully of what they will do, is not a difference of opportunity. It is a difference of spirit. The doers are fired with a determination that nothing can stagger; they are imbued with a faith that nothing can shake. — *Angelo Patri*.

Concentrating on One Stock

JUMPING all over the list of stocks has kept many a trader from making progress in his work. In trading you should be more or less of a specialist to accomplish best results. Scattered effort can never accomplish what concentrated attention will do. Carnegie used to say, "Put your eggs in one basket and watch that basket." That was really a good principle for him, and in thousands of cases of industrial life has proved to be a wise course.

Many have tried to apply it to their investments but rarely have found it a safe course. Carnegie's dictum has been demonstrated so often to be wrong that few of experience now follow him. The last four years did more to disprove his adage than a whole generation prior to 1929. The plan works best in an industry where one's whole time, attention and capital are needed in that one business.

The reason is obvious. In conducting a business, concentrated attention develops a finished organization. "This one thing I do" is generally the motto of a successful enterprise. Notable instances could be cited where the opposite course has proved disastrous.

In stock trading it has often been proved that attention on one or two, possibly three stocks is a satisfactory course to pursue. A trader would do well never to handle more stocks than he can study intensively and watch constantly. The variations of movement of three active stocks are so many that only an extraordinary mind, one of the chess expert variety, can remember for any length of time what has happened.

If you think little is happening in an active stock try this: — Keep a record of every movement all day long. From the tape put down every transaction in its relative position. You will soon see there is constant motion. Almost any stock except the most sluggish is weaving a pattern all day long and all of the time. By concentrating on not more than three stocks, you will become so familiar with their every little movement that the slightest change will have significance for you. Since every stock has particular movements growing out of circumstances back of its company as well as from general conditions, you will soon have a picture interesting and prophetic of what is just ahead. You will be able to interpret the action of these stocks far better than the casual observer. And that is all you need do to make money. Being a little more expert in discernment than others is sufficient for success.

There is a man in New York who has been concentrating on Steel for twenty-five years. He knows its every habit, idiosyncrasy and peculiarity better perhaps than any other person in America. He never buys or sells anything but this one stock, and makes money out of it all the time. Back of his work, of course, is a broad knowledge of essential trading principles. There is another man who for years has never traded in any other stock than Allied Chemical. He, too, makes much money.

If you are able to discipline yourself to resist various allurements that get you into this and that stock because "it looks good," or because you think you have "inside information," or because it appears "cheap," or for some other reason, and if you can stick to one, two or possibly three, you will greatly improve your chances for money making. It is a way that has been tried and not found wanting by a few very wise traders.

A majority of traders find it practically impossible to restrict themselves to so severe a course of action. It is but human nature to be influenced and affected by what is heard, seen and read. The experience of a few who have been able to resist temptation for promiscuous trading may prove to be a valuable hint.

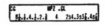

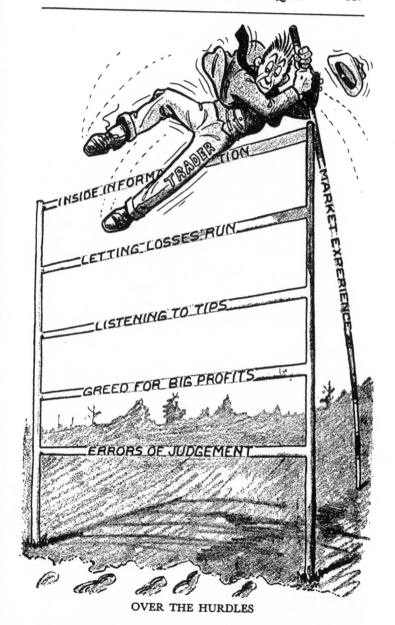

OVER THE HURDLES

The Stockbroker and His Customer

Their Mutual Rights and Obligations

By Jacob Scholer *of the New York Bar*

Third Article

Concluding Installment

The Rights of Customers Upon the Bankruptcy of the Broker

THE rights of a customer against a broker who has become bankrupt or the receiver or trustee of such a broker, and the rights in such cases of the customers, as between themselves, are frequently very difficult to determine. Sometimes the precise certificates of stock purchased for the customer are on hand, in which case the matter is comparatively simple, for then there is no question as to the customer's right to receive the stock. It will be remembered that, under the New York doctrine, title to the stock passes to the customer when it is purchased for him by the broker, and the broker merely has a lien upon the stock for his unpaid charges. Where the customer, therefore, pays the debit balance in his account, he is entitled to his securities. Where precise identification is not possible, and there is a block of stocks of the particular kind on hand, sufficient to satisfy the demand for that kind of stock of all the customers of the broker, and of the broker himself, there too the problem is simple.

Difficulties arise where the broker himself owns blocks of the particular stock, and there is an insufficient number of shares of the particular stock not capable of identification, coupled with the fact that the whole amount is insufficient to satisfy the demands of all the margin-buying customers. In such cases, as a general rule, it is held that the customers are entitled to a pro rata distribution.

The reason for some of the difficulties that arise in these situations is the conflict of interest between general unsecured creditors of the broker and the margin-buying customers. Since under the law a customer who buys stocks on margin has title to the stocks, it is now the rule that the customer is justified in redeeming his stocks from the broker by paying off his debit balance, even though the broker is insolvent at the time. This principle was upheld in the leading case of *Richardson* v. *Shaw*, 209 U. S. 365. The customer in that case had a margin account with a broker who failed. At a time when the broker was insolvent, the customer paid off his debit balance and received back the securities. It was claimed by the creditors of the bankrupt that the securities should be returned, because the return of the securities under such circumstances was preferential. The court held that the relation between a broker and his customer was that of pledgor and pledgee, and that therefore the customer having retained title to the securities was justified in paying off his debit balance and receiving back the collateral, even though the broker was insolvent at the time of the transaction.

We are living in a world of changing conditions and standards in all fields of activity. Even fundamental laws, grounded in tradition and upheld by authority, are being modified, enlarged and restricted, and laws governing the relationship of broker and customer are no exception. Recently, by enactment of Federal legislation, we have seen the rule governing the transactions between buyer and seller, particularly in regard to sales of securities, changed from Caveat Emptor — let the purchaser beware — to Caveat Vendor — let the seller beware. At the present time, further legislation is pending materially affecting transactions between the broker and his customer. If a customer trades on margin his broker is entitled to be protected to insure the payment to him of the customer's debit balance. He has the means of procuring that protection and should avail himself of those means. The customer, too, is entitled to be protected, and his rights are zealously guarded not only by governmental authorities but, despite opinion in some quarters to the contrary, by the New York Stock Exchange. I know that that body frequently, in the interests of a customer, has gone considerably further than the courts do in protecting the rights of the customer, because while the courts are guided by legal principles, the New York Stock Exchange is bound by no such limitation. The relation between the broker and his customer gives rise to mutual rights and obligations. These should be respected and adhered to by both parties and, unless they are, Caveat Broker and Caveat Customer.

The Law of Financial Success*

FIX your mind firmly upon anything, good or bad, in the world, and you attract it to you or are attracted to it in obedience to the Law. You attract to you the things you expect, think about, and hold in your Mental Attitude. This is no superstitious idea, but a firmly established, scientific, psychological fact.

* * *

Fear and the emotions that come from its being do more to paralyze useful effort, good work, and finely thought-out plans, than aught else known to man. It is the hobgoblin of the race. It has ruined the lives of thousands of people. It has destroyed the finely budding characters of men and women, and made negative individuals of them in the place of strong, reliant, courageous doers of useful things.

Worry is the oldest child of Fear. It settles down upon one's mind, and crowds out all of the developing good things to be found there. Like the cuckoo in the sparrow's nest, it destroys the rightful occupants of the mind. Laid there as an egg by its parent, Fear, Worry soon hatches out and begins to make trouble. In place of the cheerful and positive "I can and I will" harmony, Worry begins to rasp out in raucous tones: "Supposin'," "What if," "But," "I can't," "I'm unlucky," "I never could do things right," "Things never turn out right with me," and so on until all the minor notes have been sounded. It makes one sick bodily and inert mentally. It retards one's progress and is a constant stumbling block in our path upward.

* * *

To manifest Ambition fully, one must first eagerly *Desire* the thing — not a mere "wanting" or "wishing" for it, but a fierce, eager, consuming hunger which demands satisfaction. And then one must have a Will aroused — sufficiently strong to go out and get that which Desire is demanding. These two elements constitute the activity of Ambition.

Look around you at the successful men of the world in any line of human effort and endeavor, and you will see that they all have

* These Excerpts are printed by permission of the publishers of the book: Regan Pub. Co., 26 E. Van Buren St., Chicago.

Ambition strongly developed. They have the fierce craving of Desire for things, and the firm Will which will brook no interference with the satisfaction of the Desire. Study the lives of Caesar, Napoleon, and their modern counterparts, the Twentieth Century Captains of Industry, and you will see the glare of this fierce Ambition burning brightly and hotly within them.

* * *

And laudable Ambition is all right. There is enough of the good things of life in this world for all of us, if we demand them, and reach out for them. Demand causes Supply, in and under the Law, so be not afraid. Arouse your Ambition — it is a good thing and not something of which to be ashamed. Urge it on — feed it — stimulate its growth. It is not a foul weed, but a strong, vigorous, healthy plant in the garden of life, bearing more fruit than any other growing thing there.

An Oklahoman writes to his Banker

"It is impossible for me to send you a check in response to your request. My present financial condition is due to the effects of federal laws, state laws, county laws, corporation laws, by-laws, brother-in-laws, mother-in-laws, and outlaws that have been foisted upon an unsuspecting public. Through the various laws, I have been held down, held up, walked on, sat on, flattened and squeezed until I do not know where I am, what I am, or why I am.

"These laws compel me to pay a merchant's tax, capital tax, stock tax, income tax, real-estate tax, property tax, auto tax, gas tax, water tax, light tax, cigar tax, street tax, school tax, syntax, and carpet tax.

"The Government has so supervised my business that I do not know who owns it. I am suspected, expected, inspected, disrespected, examined, re-examined until all I know is that I am supplicated for money for every known need, desire or hope of the human race and, because I refuse to fall and go out and beg, borrow and steal money to give away, I am cussed and discussed, boycotted, talked to, talked about, lied to, lied about, held up, held down, and robbed until I am nearly ruined. So the only reason I am clinging to life is to see what the hell is coming next."
— *Bennett's News.*

Two Kinds of Traders

ALL the people in the world are divided into two classes: Workers and Leaners.

The Workers may be described as go-getters. The Leaners want someone else to go and get things for them. As a result, the Workers generally win and the Leaners lose.

Especially in Wall Street is leaning expensive. Those who practice it drift in and out of brokerage offices harkening to everybody's opinion, reading all the dope sheets — leaning, listening but making no real effort to learn the Wall Street machinery and how to derive profits from it. They want something for nothing.

The Workers, on the other hand, are out to achieve something, and they go hot after it. They study, investigate, practice and keep at it till they acquire a knowledge and a judgment of their own.

As William Randolph Hearst says:

"Achievement is a great thing to make your life interesting and satisfying. It is not a labor, it is a joy.

"The hope of achievement gives you an object and an occupation that intrigues you as you look ahead.

"The actual achievement, in addition to the momentary satisfaction, gives you something to look back on with permanent pleasure.

"Therefore, consider achievement not as a chore but as something to make your life pass pleasantly and profitably.

"Make up your mind what you want to do and then go out and do it.

"Make up your mind. That is the thing.

"It is astonishing what a facile and yet inflexible instrument the mind is.

"It can be set in any direction, but once securely and sincerely set it adheres to that purpose until it is achieved."

Beating the News by Reading the Tape

TRADERS who base their operations upon business statistics and other news developments have been more bewildered than ever since the New Deal went into action. If President Roosevelt himself doesn't know what decisions may be reached tomorrow, or their full consequences, how is the average trader to trim his sail to the ever shifting winds? It just can't be done by interpreting the news.

But the tape reader navigates with more efficient equipment. From close study of the market's action he can usually sense when important developments are pending, and their probable effect upon the price trend. It is not necessary for him to understand the complicated economic theories involved, nor spend hours and days reading about what other people think. The vital problem for the trader is: What construction will the market put upon the news? This he can learn in advance from the tape. It is the best kind of inside information.

Here is a striking example: The morning papers of Saturday, October 21, carried the important news that President Roosevelt was to speak over the radio Sunday evening. It was generally expected that some explanation would then be offered of his currency plans. During the short session of Saturday, prices declined and closed near the bottom. People who look to the news for their cue were generally afraid to take a position over the week-end.

President Roosevelt's Sunday evening speech announced a new gold-buying policy, which the Monday papers were at a loss to explain. Even the bankers were befuddled. Tape readers hadn't the slightest idea of what it was all about either, but noted that the action of the market before the close Saturday said that the news would be favorable and that the market would open up Monday. And the tape was right.

The Street seemed to believe that nothing could be accomplished by limiting our purchases of gold to the output of domestic mines. Wall Street was in a blue funk; but the tape said: "Buy." So tape readers bought. Wednesday brought the news that the President would purchase gold in the world markets. It took about a day for the public to decide what to make of this. Then prices began to move upward again.

For the third time within less than two weeks the tape had given sound advice in a complex situation where the trade news was discouraging, and even expert bankers and economists were not able to agree upon the effect of the President's announcement.

THE GUIDE BOOK OF EXPERIENCE

We are fools if we do not look for guidance in the book of experience.

He who would search for the lessons of experience will never reach the end. Daily he must put to the test his clearest insight into the immediate.

How, amidst this clash of insistent men, are the rest of us to find a course to follow? Only, it seems to me, by rejecting all arbitrariness of mind, whether it be the expectation of instant cures or the prophesies of certain disaster, or an unwillingness to confess error, and then by remaining collected and alert, ready to change our action as we watch for and interpret the signs and the reports. That is the way armies are directed and ships at sea are steered. — *Walter Lippman in N. Y. Herald Tribune.*

THE ROMANCE OF A STOCK MARKET

IMAGINATION — creative imagination has tunneled mountains and bridged rivers; conquered the air and seas; delved into the bowels of the earth for its treasure and devised methods and means for their greater usefulness to mankind. Imagination drives the hardy pioneer who opens the wilderness to civilization, the explorer in distant lands, the inventor poring over his test tubes or mechanisms.

* * *

Great inventions which have contributed so largely to industrial and commercial progress were all regarded at first as merely wild schemes of hare-brained cranks. The steamboat, railroad, telegraph and other great agencies of civilization were all considered the wildest of speculations in their early stages. Thousands of examples may be cited of imaginatively created projects which suffered from lack of proper attention at the beginning but which are now highly desirable and profitable investments.

* * *

Progress is the mark of civilization — it is essential. Anything which aids progress and furnishes opportunity is of vital importance to progress. The test of time tries all human institutions and only those which render an essential service survive. The Stock Exchange is such an institution.

* * *

Ideas cause progress which does not just happen — it is brought about. Every new project and improvement must first be conceived — visioned. For the successful conclusion of practical utility there is needed more than creative imagination alone. There must be also capable management — and money. Here is the necessity for enlisting coöperation of other persons for counsel and financial aid.

* * *

Ideas need money. The creator alone generally cannot obtain sufficient funds. Assistance must be enlisted. It costs money to raise money. The greater the number from whom the money is obtained and the more revolutionary the enterprise, the greater is the difficulty in selling its securities. To what agency — individual or institutional — shall the creator of a project turn for this coöperation?

Difficulties are numerous Thus has many a perfectly legitimate and highly worthy project been neglected when it should have been welcomed and fostered. Too often it has fallen into unworthy hands.

* * *

Legislators have attempted to remedy this evil. The unfortunate results have hit innocent and guilty. In restraining evils the heavy hand of repression has fallen on worthy enterprises. In the futile effort to prevent unwise speculation it has overlooked the fact that all enterprises and projects are speculations in their inception and development. Only after a successful history do they become investments. Inevitably speculation precedes investment — it is the mother of investment. Because speculation is inherent in almost every project it is hard to draw a sharp line of distinction between speculation and investment.

* * *

Initiative and creative imagination must be encouraged — not made difficult — or progress will be strangled. There is a vast surplus of money in the hands of many who can and should take risks.

* * *

It is evident there is vital need for authoritative and competent means of bringing together these complementary forces — the project and those with money. The place where intelligent speculation in worthy projects may be made and buyer and seller meet is an established market place.

* * *

It is a boon to growth and development of the world's progress that such markets should exist, places where natural resources may be translated into capital. The aid to progress is unquestionable.

* * *

When there is better public appreciation of the importance and economic value of speculative markets operated intelligently and conservatively with sound restrictions, with charges and methods standardized and quotations published daily, undue criticism and antagonism will cease and the progress of civilization be fostered.

A Small Trader Should Be a Hitch-Hiker

MANY people feel they have no opportunity to trade successfully because their supply of funds is small. They have a feeling that the forces that move prices are so powerful and oftentimes under such deliberate regulation and involve so much arbitrary and confusing manipulation, that there is no possible safety for the small trader. They have the impression the little fellow is bound to be hurt whatever he does, and that he had better stay out of the game.

The small trader loses sight of the fact that the major force at work in the market is the Law of Supply and Demand, the operation of which is independent of, and too powerful for, any individual or group of individuals to regulate or modify materially.

Even if it be admitted that at certain times and under certain conditions prices of individual stocks may be influenced temporarily, the small trader should appreciate that all of this manipulation, involving certain price swings, is conducted without personal expense to him.

The small operator often fails to realize he has the same privilege as anyone else of observing from hour to hour, day to day and week to week, manifestations of the Law of Supply and Demand as disclosed by prices and volumes on the ticker tape. If he observes these facts in sequence, he may record them, correlate them, and interpret them in a manner that will give him practically the same information as is in the possession of individuals or interests heavily committed in the market for his favorite stock. He can see accumulation or absorption of the stock from day to day, and final preparations for the upward swing. He may observe signals that are usually disclosed as the prepared move gets under way. He can do all this with practically no expense or risk. He need not help pay for the preparation for the move, nor share the expense of bringing it about.

Figuratively speaking, therefore, the small trader should imagine himself as a hitch-hiker in the market. For the ordinary hitch-hiker someone else supplies the car, chauffeur, oil and gas. When he thinks the car is about to go in his direction, he jumps aboard and rides as far as he thinks the car will go. When he notices the machine has been stopped by a red light, or is about to turn a corner and go in some other direction, or that the car is running out of gas, or the brakes failing to work properly, he steps off and figures he has secured about as long a ride as he may expect. All he has supplied in this transaction is a modest commission and whatever brains were necessary to observe and recognize the opportunity when to get on and off.

So it is in the market. The observer, whether a small trader or large operator, watches for his opportunity. When he sees a chance that offers reasonable odds in his favor, where the probability of profit far exceeds the risk, he buys, limits his risk and awaits developments. So long as the stock behaves properly, in accordance with technical action that confirms his original judgment, he maintains his position. As soon as he finds the stock has reached its indicated objective, approximately, or begins to waver in its stride, or passes through a set of maneuvers that clearly indicate supply is increasing, and a reactionary movement seems imminent, he acts on the information thrust upon his attention and gets out.

The small trader has some distinct advantages over the large operator. The latter usually has a position too large to liquidate suddenly at any specific price, but he must maneuver in and out of such a position. Sometimes this means considerable loss of profit because of insufficient demand to meet his particular supply. On the other hand, the small trader can nearly always be assured of a price close to the market at the time he decides to sell.

One Variety of "Experts"

AN experienced trader from the Middle West says this: "Years ago when associated with an advisory service, I came to the conclusion that Wall Street is a fertile field for a doctor of psychopathy. The number of self-styled "experts" who drifted into my office with new-fangled ideas for beating the market without the use of ordinary gray matter, was really amazing. Their attitude might have been funny but for the fact that they were too often annoying. Their strong suit was an air of mystery and a blustering front. Every one had discovered the great secret, how to make money by a sure-fire system which didn't require any effort. Of course, these systems were the result of "years of intensive research." That was quite apparent from the shiny state of deponents' trousers and the battered condition of their chapeaux.

The Street perennially yields a crop of these impractical seekers after substitutes for judgment. The latest harvest of these "technicians" includes a class of "authorities" on "gaps" and "laps." Some proponents of the "gap" theory say the theory is not fully perfected because vertical line or bar charts were developed only over the last few years.

Here is a bit of real news for old-time, experienced traders. The "experts" have discovered something.

They have thus far succeeded in capturing enough species of gaps to classify them biologically. They are to be known by such intriguing titles as "breakaway," "exhaustion," and "measuring." Rules that have been devised for classifying such phenomena are suggestive of the Chinese alphabet and just as practical for the average trader. They tell us that once the rules have been learned the rest is easy. So we are told to buy when we see an "exhaustion" gap, and sell when we get the "breakaway." But be careful we don't get confused, or the margin clerk will do the "measuring."

The Trader's Insurance

MANY people complain that their stop orders are nearly always caught. There is good reason for this. They make their trades at the wrong times. Their stops are not correctly placed. They usually buy on bulges and sell on weakness. Naturally there are reactions after bulges and rallies after weakness and these secondary moves catch their stops. Besides, there is a certain science in timing one's trades, as well as in placing stops; knowledge of this yields a large percentage in one's favor.

Some day the Stock Exchange may pass a rule prohibiting its members from calling clients for margin; making it compulsory, when the client's equity is depreciated that the broker insist on his closing out some of his trades. Thus his remaining margin will be sufficient. That may seem a little radical, but it would be best for brokers and clients. The great stock market calamities suffered by the public are due almost solely to the fact that losses are rarely limited except by the purses and bank accounts of traders and so-called investors. If everyone who was long of the market in the summer of 1929 had limited his risk to two, three, five or even ten points from the prices at which purchases were made there would have been no panic! At no stage in the decline need anyone have flung caution to the winds and liquidated his holdings at whatever he could get. It was the stampede of selling "at the market" that produced the panic; for a panic after all is merely a state of mind in which millions of people trample each other in their endeavor to get out at any price.

Chance and the Stock Market
PART I

THERE is much loose talk about luck and the stock market. If a trader is successful, some people are prone to disparage his ability by calling it luck. A "boob" excuses his losses by asserting he happened to be unlucky. Persistent losers driven by desperation have been known to flip a coin as a means of deciding whether to buy or sell.

It is understandable, perhaps, that the general public, which has made no serious study of this highly scientific business, should look upon stock trading as a game of chance. There appeared recently an astounding article by a market research worker who ought to know better proclaiming such views. Some of the statements made are these:

"The Stock Market is a creature of pure chance."

"If chance rules the stock market, how can one profit? The question might just as properly be worded; How does the banker of a roulette profit?"

"You can win only when you are willing to believe that the next move in stocks is not predictable."

The author professes ability to satisfactorily amplify these ideas. Standing alone such views are amusing to those who are well informed on the subject. They know that price movements in the stock market are predictable in greater or lesser degree because they are governed by the inexorable law of Supply and Demand, not by mere chance. If chance ruled the market, altogether different basic conceptions would have to be used than now govern. The nature of the laws of chance are such that neither persistent losses or profits can be explained on the ground of pure luck.

There are traders who make money year in and year out without access to "inside information." Were making or losing money a matter of pure luck a trader might be right about as often as wrong over a long period.

The Trader's Paradise Is Now

PROBABLY no more frequent complaint is heard from time to time than that the market is too slow, inactive and narrow for anyone to make money. For four months previous to the convening of Congress, this was a common lament. Traders lounged idly over their tickers and tapes, and almost everyone who was watching the market agreed with everyone else that there was "nothing doing"; that stocks could get nowhere because restrictions were to be imposed on traders; because severe limitations were being put upon the operations of pools; because the President would not declare himself in favor of stabilization; and so on endlessly.

Did those registering these complaints stop and think that the market is *always* beset by conditions that make for uncertainty? Every day has its market balance sheet, consisting of favorable and unfavorable elements. Were it not for this, prices would go in only one direction. If everything were gloriously good and happy there would be a bull market forever, theoretically. And if all were gloom and despair eternally, stocks would simply disappear from the market place.

But the more uncertain conditions are, the more often does the tape afford opportunities; the more definitely is the trader's skill tested, and the greater the possible profits to be gleaned.

According to analysis of the small daily fluctuations, an invaluable auxiliary to scientific trading, there are frequent days when the market makes from six to twelve turns. Any sensitive index of market activity shows a constant weaving motion of the leading stocks. And these motions of the leaders are followed in some degree by nearly every stock on the list.

Follow this aid closely and you will see that the market travels over many points in the course of every five-hour session. Up and down prices are always swinging all day long, sometimes in ten-minute intervals, sometimes in two-hour intervals, but averaging about a half hour. The alert trader has in this a Utopia for profits.

A seemingly slow market is only a matter of the distance at which you view the picture. If you look at the ocean from a five-mile height, you cannot discern the billows that are tossing. It looks like a flat surface. Get down on the shore and you will see the big and little waves.

It is so with the stock market. When conditions are uncertain, it is jumpy and active nearly every day, and all day long. At such times it is a veritable trader's paradise.

Stock Market Glossary

TAPE: A worm that never turns.

A CALL: A request for more margin.

THE STREET: Where you land unless you know how.

BULL: The come-on stuff handed out by "authorities."

MARKET LETTER WRITER: One who tells you what he knows in a few lines.

STATISTICIAN: A guy who has the right figures but the wrong company.

A PUT: Usually followed by "out." What you get when you have no more money.

TRADER: A chap who puts stop loss orders on his stocks so he can cancel them.

MARGIN CLERK: A human owl who can't see a thing in the daytime but keeps you awake all night.

BEAR: Usually misspelt — should be BARE. The state in which your bank account and your wardrobe will be left, if you don't learn the rules.

OFFICE BOY: The only wise guy in the office. He takes his money home and gives it to his mother.

High Spots
In a Wall Street Career

This condensed series is from Mr. Wyckoff's autobiography
"Wall Street Ventures and Adventures Through 40 years."
It will be continued through several more issues.

1906   A Shift in Trend

ONE of the interesting incidents while I was at Wasserman's was Mr. Keene's raid on Metropolitan Securities. This stock, by which control of the traction situation in New York City was held, had been pegged for a long time at 50; it would fluctuate between 50 and 53. The pool never allowed it to break below 50. Whenever it approached 50, traders and specialists would buy it, and whenever it went to 53 or 54 they would sell it short.

One afternoon a sudden activity broke out in the stock. Large lots of it began to come out on the tape at reduced prices. At about a quarter of three Dave Lamar, known as "The Wolf of Wall Street," came into the office, sat down at the ticker, and began telling us Mr. Keene was going to "smash that Metropolitan Securities" this time. He and his friends were giving the pool a bellyful, and tomorrow morning it would open away down.

Eddie Wasserman, and others there, decided to help the game along and sold some round lots. Lamar's relationship with Keene was well known. What he was telling us in our office he had told, and would tell, others. Mr. Keene, having sold his own lines short before the joyful news was spread, was taking this method of getting all the help he could. What with Keene's generalship and Lamar's advertising of what Keene was going to do to the stock, the pool had about all they wanted by three o'clock that afternoon. And the next morning, as there was no knowing how much selling was still coming from the same source, the stock opened below 50 and then cracked down another dozen points into the 30s, realizing profits for all hands.

This was an impressive lesson in the law of supply and demand: Supply, *actual* the day before, and *threatened* on the following day, discouraged August Belmont and his associates, who were on the supporting side, and put another feather in the cap of the man to whom the newspapers used to refer as "a prominent operator" — Mr. Keene.

* * *

Wasserman Bros. opened a branch office in London, in charge of Blakeley Hall, a friend of Dick Canfield. The office, at No. 2 Cockspur Street, needed a lot of fixing, and I was sent over there to help get him started. A short time after I arrived, Hall and the firm began an argument by cable, and as Hall threatened to quit unless his demands were met, I could make no further progress and took the next steamer back home, having been absent seventeen days. Wasserman offered me the management of the London office but I declined it, and not long after that decided to resign. I had learned what I wanted to learn here, and it had become my habit to avoid ruts.

When I told Eddie of my decision he said: "Why do you want to quit? I like you. You can stay here twenty-five years!"

I told him I was rather fed up on the brokerage business and wanted to get into bonds and unlisted securities for myself.

I went down Exchange Place and engaged a small room at No. 43. Then around to the Bank of the Manhattan Company to see its president, Stephen L. Baker, who knew me through my silent partnership in Price, McCormick & Co. and the thousands of checks I had signed on his bank. Mr. Wasserman had also given me a splendid letter to him.

I told Mr. Baker I was going to start a bond business under the name of Wyckoff & Co., that I would be alone in the enterprise, that my initial deposit would be $20,000. Also that I would clear my own transactions, and for that purpose would like to have him over-certify my checks to the amount of $100,000. This he granted me.

I started doing business, and soon was making much more money than at Wasserman's, mostly trading in bonds and unlisted securities, without attempting to work up an investment clientele.

* * *

Early in 1906, a conference (so I was told by one who said he had attended it) of the Harriman-Standard Oil party had been held at the house of John D. Rockefeller at Lakewood, N. J. Measures were determined upon with the aim of inducing the public to buy in a volume which would create a market on which these large operators could successfully unload.

Union Pacific was then selling above 150. The plan was to put it on a 10 per cent basis and at the same time establish Southern Pacific as a 5 per cent stock. This, it was expected, would have the desired effect.

Union Pacific was therefore backed down to 139, and heavy accumulation took place. Then one morning, some time after the opening, one or two members of the New York Stock Exchange, happening to glance on the bulletin board on the floor, saw to their amazement that Union Pacific stood announced there as a 10 per cent stock and Southern Pacific as a 5 per cent. Union Pacific jumped to the 190s in a few days and Southern Pacific from the lower 60s into the 90s almost as quickly. This Union Pacific deal produced the climax of the 1906 bull market in which the average price of twenty rails reached 168, a figure not again touched for many years. Following this tremendous rise, in which Harriman made $15,000,000 on his speculative line of Union Pacific alone, the dominating stock market operators, and many of the leading financiers, banks and banking institutions who read the handwriting on the wall, were able to clean house.

1907   The Money Panic

At the beginning of this year the outlook was ominous. Liquid capital, absorbed by the tremendous financial operations, promotions, and consolidations of the past years had shrunk everywhere — in America and the world over. Jacob H. Schiff, of Kuhn, Loeb & Co., had already sounded a warning. Failure to revise the banking laws and provide a more elastic currency, he had said, would eventually precipitate the worst panic this country had ever seen.

Foreign wars, the Baltimore fire, the San Francisco earthquake and fire, had absorbed $2,000,000,000 of liquid capital, tying up four times that amount of credit.

Through certain channels of information I ascertained that many large estates which held tremendous holdings of railroad securities had split up the certificates running into tens and hundreds of thousands of shares and were liquidating.

Banks were steadily calling in loans. Time money was hard to get. Business was bad. So was the stock market. No one knew just what was going to happen and all those who dealt in stocks — investors, bankers and brokers — were uneasy.

The great shrinkage in security values and the almost total loss of confidence in the financial world resulting from President Roosevelt's campaign against the capitalists who had attempted to consolidate the great transportation systems, was followed by a period of state and federal attacks upon corporations. Financiers crawled into their shells.

Large railroad systems, in process of extension and development, found it difficult to obtain money, even at high rates. Strong companies like New York Central and Pennsylvania were forced to resort to short-term notes. Weaker systems found it almost impossible to finance themselves at all. The railroad outlook was such as to scare both railroad men and investors in their bonds and shares.

Early in the year Mr. Morgan had called upon President Roosevelt at Washington to warn him of the dangers of the situation; suggested he have a meeting of all the leading railroad heads with the President. But Roosevelt was determined to proceed on his aggressive course regardless of the effect upon finance, transportation and business. He did not seem to care what damage was done through the country so long as he should succeed in putting "certain malefactors of great wealth" where he wanted them.

The first section of the panic, following this conference, came in March. Roosevelt blamed Wall Street, and Wall Street blamed Roosevelt.

During the summer another break in the stock market carried prices to new lows. The $29,000,000 fine against the Standard Oil Company was announced. The United States Attorney General was giving interviews to newspaper men. He thought of himself as a hunter. He spoke of "a big covey of game of which he proposed to land a bird or two." The President was issuing statements to the effect that Wall Street was attempting to discredit his administration.

Along in October banks in New York City and elsewhere began to fail; this was followed by runs upon all kinds of financial institutions throughout the land. Cash commanded a premium of 4 to 5 per cent; that is, you could take a thousand dollars in bills to any bank in New York and get in return a check for $1,040 or $1,050. With varying fluctuations this condition kept on for the last three months of the year.

At one time in November the Clearing House banks showed a deficiency of over $54,000,000 in their normal reserve requirements. The Knickerbocker Trust Co. paid out $8,000,000 in deposits and then failed. The Trust Co. of America, paying off only a few depositors an hour, was emptied of $23,000,000 before the run stopped. Long lines of depositors stood, all day and all night, at the paying tellers' windows of many banks in New York City. Wall Street was jammed from curb to curb with an excited mob.

Finally, there was no money at all for members of the New York Stock Exchange who wanted to borrow. Then J. P. Morgan stepped in to save the situation. Forming a money pool, he authorized the loaning of $27,000,000 to brokers on the floor of the Exchange. This turned the tide, but it was a long while before money, banking and stock market conditions became normal again.

The action of Union Pacific during that time was typical of what was happening in the market. After reaching its high point of 195⅜ in September, 1906, this stock had declined nearly 20 points in October, and had rallied into December. Then followed a series of further slumps in January and February, 1907, until after March 14, the low point of the first half of the panic, the stock was down to 120, or 75 points under its record high.

Rallies and slumps succeeded each other — 10, 20 or 30 points — up into May. Another slump and a rise took up the month of June and part of July; and in August the stock was back nearly to 120.

It was a sick market with the nausea not completed. I should judge that along about then Union Pacific, still a $10 per annum dividend payer, was reaccumulated to the limit of the resources of the Harriman party, for when later, on October 24, the panic had reached its worst and Union Pacific at its low was par, Harriman was walking the floor in Morgan's office muttering: "Union Pacific at a hundred dollars per share and nobody with a dollar to buy it!"

* * *

One day I received word that James R. Keene would like to see me at the Waldorf that evening.

Visitors who called when he was in consultation in the parlor were shown into his bedroom. Nothing in the suite indicated that the occupant was the leading stock market operator and a multi-millionaire. There were a few ordinary hotel pictures on the walls. The furniture was the usual Waldorf furniture. A photograph of himself was on his chiffonier. There was no other photograph: he was evidently his own best friend.

The business was this. Keene, through his son-in-law, Mr. Taylor, had become interested in an electrical typesetting machine known as the Graphotype. He had begun by lending some money to the company and had ended by owning it. Meanwhile, the machine had been developed to high efficiency and was now ready for manufacture. He wanted me to secure subscriptions to an underwriting syndicate for an offering that was to be brought out in the Curb Market. He offered me a cash commission of 5 per cent on the amount raised and a bonus in common stock.

* * * *

We went over the Graphotype deal at length and finally reached a definite understanding. The public stenographer was called from downstairs and a contract was drawn up and signed by us both.

In undertaking to raise this money I first approached the people with whom Mr. Keene was supposed to be friendly, or at least on good business terms, and was rather surprised by the reception I received. People like George W. Perkins of J. P. Morgan & Company, Thomas Fortune Ryan, August Belmont did not seem to be interested in the least. They seemed to think the proposition a rather unusual one for Mr. Keene, who had been identified with such great operations in the stock market as the distribution of Amalgamated Copper and U. S. Steel. He had never promoted a stock of his own, and here he was working to bring out on the Curb an enterprise capitalized at only a million or two. Belmont had his secretary telephone Keene, as the latter afterward told me, to see whether this was really his enterprise, and a lot of the others simply wouldn't go in at all. Perkins told me it was too small for J. P. Morgan & Co. Perhaps they suspected that Keene might unload on the syndicate the package he had been carrying, in which he had several hundred thousand dollars.

Other installments will follow

Watch the Whole Market

THE action of the whole market tells you when the selling is
better than the buying and vice versa. You do not care *why*
insiders are buying or selling, but you should care a lot about the
action of their stock on the tape, for that is what tells you the truth.

The action of a single stock is its own best forecaster.

When you know how to read the tape and interpret the action of
the whole market and of individual stocks, you will be "on the
ground floor" with the insiders, without having anything to do with
them. That is because the tape tells the real story. To become a successful trader, you must learn to judge by the action of the market.
It is the action of the market which carries the greatest influence
with insiders.

Behind the Scenes

In Room 267 of the Treasury, behind a black velvet curtain,
three tickers furiously spattered paper tape with symbols all day
long. At an oval mahogany table Archibald Lockheed, exchange
expert, and five assistants studied the tapes, drew red and black
lines on graph paper, and prepared reports to be submitted to
Secretary Morgenthau every evening so that he could plan the next
day's exchange operations. — *National Affairs.*

There Are Four Kinds of Men

He that knows not and knows not that he knows not is a
fool — shun him;

He that knows not and knows that he knows not is weak —
pity him;

He that knows and knows not that he knows is asleep —
wake him;

He that knows and knows that he knows is wise — follow
him. — *Arabian Proverb.*